OTHER
INDIAN EVENTS
OF
NEW ENGLAND

PRESENTED BY THE

STATE STREET TRUST
COMPANY

THE FIRST AMERICAN THANKSGIVING, PLYMOUTH, MASSACHUSETTS

That first long severe winter of 1620 caused much illness and many deaths among the recently arrived Pilgrims. The crops proved abundant in the following autumn, and so Governor Bradford of the Massachusetts Colony decided to declare a three-day feast and celebration, followed by sports between the English and the Indians, during October of 1621. This repast consisted of wild turkeys, geese, ducks, fish, corn bread and vegetables. Massasoit and other Indians, to be seen at the right of the picture, were present and contributed four deer. This gathering has been called our First American Thanksgiving, but was not continued at all regularly until many years afterwards.

OTHER INDIAN EVENTS
OF
NEW ENGLAND

A Collection of INTERESTING INCIDENTS
in the LIVES of the EARLY SETTLERS
and the Indians of this Country
with Reproductions of OLD PRINTS
and PHOTOGRAPHS

VOLUME II
Compiled by ALLAN FORBES

The mark of Caunannicus
[Canonicus]

ISSUED BY THE
STATE STREET TRUST COMPANY
OF BOSTON
in Commemoration of its Fiftieth
Anniversary

1941

Ent. Sept. 13, 1949

*The statue of the mounted
Indian reproduced on the cover of
this brochure stands in front of the Museum
of Fine Arts, Boston, and is entitled "The Appeal
to the Great Spirit." The sculptor is Cyrus E. Dallin, who
is famous for his great work, especially that
relating to Indians. Reproduced by
courtesy of Mr. Dallin.*

*Arranged and printed by direction of
Walton Advertising & Printing Co.
Boston, Mass.*

PRINTED IN U. S. A.

FOREWORD

THE year 1941 marks the Golden Anniversary of the State Street Trust Company. We at first considered issuing a booklet descriptive of fifty years of the Bank's history, but after due reflection we thought it would be of more interest to our depositors and other readers if we published an historical pamphlet similar in character to the series of twenty-eight issued over the past thirty-five years. In 1934 we published a story of the New England Indians and, as there was much valuable material remaining, we have concluded to print a second volume on the same subject. As before, we have confined ourselves chiefly to peaceful events, believing that there is much to relate outside of the conflicts that took place from time to time, which have been so frequently recorded.

Fifty years in itself is not a long time in the world's history, yet during that period the Trust Company hopes it has made a useful place for itself in New England, and believes it has been able to accumulate considerable knowledge of banking and trust problems for the benefit of its patrons, of whom, we are pleased to say, we have a large number in our different departments. In addition to the knowledge gained by our own staff, we have been greatly benefited by the experience of the National Union Bank, which was chartered in 1792, and which became a part of our institution in 1925, carrying the bank interests back for one hundred and forty-nine years. The Paul Revere Trust Company joined the Trust Company in 1916, thereby adding some valuable connections, and still more recently, in 1936, the Union Trust Company, of which Charles Francis Adams was the President, merged with this Bank, creating a well-rounded institution, and bringing some valuable officers, clerks and connections to our banking, trust and safe deposit departments. Our bank was chartered as the State Street Safe Deposit & Trust Company and began business on July 1, 1891. The first day's deposits totalled $8,898.20 in nine accounts. Our first trust came to us during our first year, on February 27, 1892. Our first dividend was paid April 1, 1892, and dividends have been paid without interruption ever since.

The name of the bank was changed to State Street Trust Company in March of 1897, the change bearing the official approval of Governor Roger Wolcott, the father of our present Senior Vice President, Samuel H. Wolcott.

Our first branch office was opened February 1, 1902, on Massachusetts Avenue and our present building, at the corner of Massachusetts Avenue and Boylston Street, was opened on November 20, 1905, which happened to be the writer's birthday. Our Copley Square Office at 581 Boylston Street came to us with the Paul Revere Trust Company in 1916; and our Union Trust Office, 24 Federal Street, is the former office of the Union Trust Company, which merged with us, as stated previously, in 1936.

We have always believed and hoped that our historical monographs which have been carefully prepared, with their stories and pictures, might tend to show the public that equal care is used in our efforts to furnish the best of service and attention to the wants of our present customers, and those who may decide to avail themselves of our services.

We wish to express our appreciation to the following persons who have assisted us in the preparation of this brochure: William Alcott, Joseph C. Allen, H. P. Ayer, J. Robert Bentley, Clarence S. Brigham, Arthur W. Brown, the late Howard M. Chapin, William H. Claflin, Jr., the late Captain John A. Cook, Frank H. Damon, Mrs. Ozias Dodge, Miles H. Dustin, Dr. Samuel A. Eliot, Mrs. Raymond Emerson, R. F. Haffenreffer, John W. Haley, Albert H. Hall, Albert C. Harding, the late P. LeRoy Harwood, Mrs. Anna L. Hayson, Wallis E. Howe, Frank Walcott Hutt, Lawrence W. Jenkins, Joshua H. Jones, Harold D. Kilgore, G. E. E. Lindquist, Willard B. Luther, the late William F. Macy, Francis I. McCanna, Frank Nichols, Edward F. O'Dowd, Rev. Charles E. Park, Mabel Parmenter, Arthur L. Peale, Philip J. Potter, F. L. Richardson, Ernest E. Rogers, George L. Rockwell, the late Albert L. Sawyer, Miss Clara Endicott Sears, Earle W. Stamm, Rev. Thomas E. Thompson, George H. Tripp, W. S. Trowbridge, Harry B. Turner, Maurice W. Turner, M.D., Julius H. Tuttle, the late Rev. Wilson Waters, the late Walter K. Watkins, Frederic Earle Whitaker and the late Frederic Winthrop.

We wish also to express our appreciation to the staff of the Boston Public Library, who have been very helpful and patient in furnishing us with reference books for use in our research. We have found their whole-hearted co-operation a very important factor in our work.

Our thanks are also due to the officials and members of the staffs of the following libraries and historical societies: Chelmsford Historical Society, Connecticut Historical Society, Connecticut State Library, Rhode Island Historical Society, Providence Public Library, John Carter Brown Library, George L. Shepley Library, Harvard College Library, Haverhill Public Library and Woonsocket Historical Society.

The Trust Company also wishes to acknowledge the devoted efforts of Miss Katherine G. Rogers in typing the manuscript and the considerable volume of correspondence necessary in having the material checked by those familiar with the various chapters, and of Miss Helen M. Johnson (now Mrs. John M. Foley, Jr.), who gave much time in assisting in the typewriting involved.

The author also desires to recognize the help given by Ralph M. Eastman, Vice President of the Trust Company, in carefully reviewing the manuscript and for helpful suggestions made in the preparation of the material here presented.

Perry Walton and his efficient staff, as in previous years, arranged and printed the brochure, which we trust will prove to be a fitting addition to the series already published.

ALLAN FORBES,
President, State Street Trust Company.

Boston, 1941.

TABLE OF CONTENTS

	PAGE
Governor Winthrop and His Indian Visitors	1
Nantucket and the Indian	14
The Indian at the Vineyard	24
Indian Games	30
Journey Cake — Jonny-Cake	39
Queen Awashonks	40
King Philip and the Taunton Treaty	45
Natick and Nonantum	48
Indians Interned on Deer Island	57
Harvard and the Indian	64
Hannah Dustin of Haverhill	77
Indian Reminders in Rhode Island and Connecticut (*By pictures*)	87

The marke of the Squa [Squaw] Sachem Awashunckes [Awashonks]

The mark of Miantinomu [Miantonomo]

Chickatabutt [Chickatabot] allies [alias] Josias his marke

King Philip His Mark

A FEW INDIAN SIGNATURES

vii

TABLET ON THE FOUNDERS' MEMORIAL ON THE BEACON STREET MALL OF BOSTON COMMON

In commemoration of the Three Hundredth Anniversary of the founding of Boston in the year 1630. It shows the meeting of William Blaxton (left), the first white settler in Boston, with Governor John Winthrop (right), who removed from Charlestown across Charles River to the shore opposite. This event was the first important act in the founding of this city. Blaxton is seen touching hands with Winthrop, for in those days people did not shake hands. Behind the Governor, with a Bible under his arm, is Reverend John Wilson, first minister of the First Church, and next to him is the Puritan maiden, Ann Pollard, the first woman to set foot on the shores of Boston. Boatmen are seen hauling up on the beach the rowboats in which the party came over, and the ship is the *Arbella*. At the left, symbolizing their friendship and helpfulness to the early settlers, is a group of friendly Indians who accompanied Blaxton. This memorial is placed over the spring from which Blaxton got his water supply, which induced Winthrop and his followers to remove here. Blaxton's house was situated opposite, on the corner of Beacon and Spruce Streets. Frank G. Allen, then Governor of Massachusetts (now a Director of our Trust Company) Charles Francis Adams (now Chairman of our Board) and Mayor Curley made addresses, and the writer was a member of the Committee. Miss Katherine Winthrop, a direct descendant of Governor Winthrop, unveiled the memorial on September 16, 1930. Among the many celebrities present at the dedication ceremony was Reuben Salter, Mayor of Boston, England.

Other

INDIAN EVENTS
of NEW ENGLAND

GOVERNOR WINTHROP AND HIS INDIAN VISITORS

OVERNOR John Winthrop and his colonists were brought into early contact with the Indians of Massachusetts, for on the very day of their arrival in Salem Harbour on June 12, 1630, according to Winthrop's diary, "An Indian came aboard us and lay there all night." Salem was then known as Naumkeag and was spelled by him "Nahumkeck." The Puritans must have been a little disconcerted to have a strange redskin spend the night on the *Arbella*, and were doubtless much relieved to have him depart the next morning. A day or two later Winthrop records that Masconomo, the Sagamore of Agawam, now Ipswich, and one of his men came aboard and stayed all day. Three days later, on the seventeenth, the fleet set sail for "Mattachusetts, to find out a place for our sitting down," to quote again from this diary. It may be of interest to mention that Masconomo was buried in Hamilton on Sagamore Hill, which so much resembles the Scotch moors.

The next Indian visitor received by the Governor was the well-known Chickatabot, who came to Boston on March 23rd of the following year with a present of a hogshead of Indian corn. At this time Winthrop had moved from his "Great House" in Charlestown, to a newer abode on State Street on the site of the Exchange Building, the present home of the State Street Trust Company. Chickatabot, meaning "House-a-fire," the chief Sagamore of Massachusetts, was one of the earliest Indians connected with the history of Dorchester, and had his chief seat not far from the Neponset River at Moswetuset Hummock, or Sachem's Knoll, opposite the Dennison flying field in Squantum. He was of the Wampanoag tribe and is supposed to have paid tribute to Massasoit. Ten years before, with eight other Sachems, he had made a treaty with the Pilgrims. He again assured the English of his friendship, and this action caused the newcomers to be less apprehensive and finally influenced them to abandon their recent plan of building a fortified town at Newtown, now Cambridge. The colonists had just moved to Boston and were doubtless pleased to remain where they were. Chickatabot therefore was somewhat responsible for making Boston the seat of the government. As Winthrop further explains: "After they had all dined, and had each a small cup of sack and beer, and the men tobacco, he sent away all his men and women (though the governour would have stayed them, in regard of the rain and thunder). Himself and one squaw and one sannop stayed all night, and being in English clothes, the governour set him at his own

Photographed from "Historical Markers." Erected by Massachusetts Bay Colony Tercentenary Commission

Reproduced by permission of Hon. Frederic W. Cook, Secretary of the Commonwealth of Massachusetts

MARKER POINTING TO MOSWETUSET HUMMOCK, ONE OF THE SEATS OF CHICKATABOT, AT QUINCY, MASSACHUSETTS

This piece of land, once an island, is located at the junction of Squantum Road and Wollaston Beach Boulevard, and directly opposite the Dennison Flying Field. At the left end of the knoll is a tablet recording this fact.

table where he behaved himself as soberly etc. as an Englishman. The next day after dinner he returned home, the governour giving him cheese and pease and a mug and some other small things." (The modern word for "sannop" would be "buck.") This meal which the sombre Puritans in their Old World costumes shared with the uncultivated aborigines of New England offers a strange contrast not often appreciated by the people of today. During the autumn of that same year Chickatabot again appeared to enter a complaint to the effect that one Josias Plaistowe and two of his servants had stolen corn from him. The court ordered that the culprit henceforth be addressed as "Josias" and not "Mr." He was also fined and his men whipped.

Three days later Sagamore James and his brother, Sagamore John, as they were often called, sons of Nanepashemet, mentioned later, "with divers sannops" approached the governor to obtain a letter to Emanuel Downing of London, brother-in-law of Winthrop, to seek recompense for twenty beaver skins "forced" from them by a man named Watts who had returned to England. The former Indian, James, was known among his countrymen by the name of Montowampate and was sagamore of Lynn and Marblehead. It is believed he actually made a journey to England to obtain his due. The brother was called Wonohaquaham of Winisimet, anciently known as Rumney Marsh, now part of Chelsea and Saugus. He complained that two of his wigwams had been burned, and the Court ascertained that a servant of Sir Richard Saltonstall had been the culprit, whereupon the master was ordered to make satisfaction by the payment of seven yards of cloth. These two Indian brothers were friends of the English and became converted to Christianity before their death by smallpox in 1633. It is related that during one of Winthrop's visits to his farm in Mistick he wandered off after supper in quest of a wolf. It became late and as he accidentally ran across Sagamore John's empty house he decided to spend the night there. His friends at home became alarmed at his absence and the servants "shot off pieces and hallooed in the night" for him, as his account reads.

2

On April 4th of that same year Boston had a visitation from a "Quonehtacut" or Connecticut Sachem called Wahginnacut, chief of the Podunk tribe, who came here with his interpreter called Jackstraw, and Sagamore John and others. This Sachem requested Governor Winthrop to send some of his followers to plant in his country, offering presents of corn and skins as inducements. They were entertained at dinner but did not receive any encouragement from their host, as he distrusted his visitors. The Indian interpreter may possibly have been either Wanchese or Manteo, both of whom were taken to England from Virginia. One of these natives was supposed to have been a servant for Sir Walter Raleigh in England, and then to have "turned Indian" again.

Chickatabot was evidently so pleased with his first interview with the Boston officials that he repeated his visit a few weeks later, on April 13th. He also must have been much impressed with the English clothes, for he told the Governor he wished to buy a suit for himself. He was informed that "English sagamores did not used to truck" (meaning barter). The Governor nevertheless called in his tailor and gave him an order for a suit, whereupon the Indian visitor made his host a present of two large skins of coat beaver. Dinner was served to Chickatabot and his friends, after which the sachem departed saying that he would return in three days for his new outfit. Either believing the tailor would finish the clothes sooner than he promised or else being very anxious to try them on, or perhaps to get another repast, he came back at the end of two days. Winthrop, according to his own words, "put him into a very good new suit from head to foot," which is said to have fitted well; "and after he set meat before them; but he would not eat till the governour had given thanks, and after meat he desired him to do the like, and so departed." Chickatabot evidently knew that the Puritans gave thanks before meals and so refused to partake of the food until grace had been said. At the close of the meal, as pointed out by Charles J. Douglas, referring to the Dorchester Indians, the visitor went his host one better by insisting that thanks again be given. "Thus," he adds, "did a Dorchester Indian exemplify the red man's idea of the courtesy due from a guest. Has the modern aristocrat improved greatly on the ideas of social behaviour as shown by Chickatabot, the seventeenth century Indian?" Not many days later he was ordered to pay a fine of a beaver skin to satisfy some injuries done to a pig and some cattle belonging to the English. It is interesting, and at the same time astonishing, to notice that a servant of Mr. Cradock, for invectives against the church, was ordered by this same court to be whipped, to have his ears cut off, and to be banished.

Chickatabot was probably one of the "three next sagamores" that Winthrop mentioned as having been sent for at the time the colonists were concerned over rumors of war, in the autumn of 1632. This was the last visit this Massachusetts sachem made to the Governor's house, for he died of smallpox the following year, 1633, as did so many of his tribe. It is curious to read that the Puritans, many of whom cared for the Indians during this scourge, rarely caught the disease. Winthrop reports that only two English families contracted it from their Indian friends. According to some Indians, this plague is sup-

From a photograph by Ralph M. Eastman

TABLET ON MOSWETUSET HUM-MOCK, QUINCY, MASSACHUSETTS, ONE OF CHICKATABOT'S SEATS

posed to have been sent because an Indian once made the bragging remark that they were so numerous that "God could not kill them." One of the Blue Hills, from which Massachusetts got her name, is called Chickatabot in memory of this chieftain who lived not far away.

On July 13, 1631, a son of Canonicus, probably Mixanno, with Sagamore John, came to the Governor's house in State Street, where dinner was served and presents exchanged. They spent the night there and left for Narragansett shores the following day. Mixanno married Quaiapen, also known as Magnus, a daughter of the famous Ninigret. Canonicus, the great leader of the Narragansetts, was hostile to the Pilgrims for a short time after their arrival and incensed the English by waging war upon Massasoit and the Wampanoags. During the early days of the Pilgrims he sent a challenge to Plymouth in the form of a bundle of arrows bound in a rattlesnake skin. Bradford, to his surprise, returned it full of powder and bullets. Roger Williams, by his friendship with Canonicus, was able to bring an end to the bad feeling. During the Pequot war the English sought Williams' friendship and he thus wrote to Winthrop, "Sir, if anything be sent to the princes I find Canonicus would gladly accept a box of eight or ten pounds of sugar, and indeed told me he would thank Mr. Governor for a box full." Williams referred to this sachem as loving him "as his son to his last gasp." Canonicus occasionally sent presents to both Governor and Mrs. Winthrop. Drake quotes a passage from a poem published in Boston in 1803 by John Lathrop concerning Canonicus —

> "A mighty prince, of venerable age,
> A peerless warrior, but of peace the friend;
> His breast a treasury of maxims sage —
> His arm, a host — to punish or defend."

Of his death, which took place at the advanced age of eighty-four, these few lines tell:

> "I die — my friends, you have no cause to grieve:
> To abler hands my regal power I leave.
> Our God commands — to fertile realms I haste,
> Compared with which your gardens are a waste.
>
> There in full bloom eternal spring abides,
> And swarming fishes glide through azure tides,
> Continual sunshine gilds the cloudless skies,
> No mists conceal Keesuckquand [Sun God] from our eyes."

Another important sachem, destined to play an unfortunate, yet momentous, rôle in New England history was Miantonomo, the great leader of the Narragansett tribe and nephew of Canonicus. He visited Boston on August 3, 1632, with his squaw and a retinue of twelve sannops, and spent two nights in town. Of their stay here we will let Governor Winthrop tell his own story. On August 5th, "being present at the sermon, three of his sanapps went, in the meantime, and brake into a neighbor's house, etc.," being very hungry. The Governor complained to the sachem "and with some difficulty caused him to make one of his sanapps to beat them, and then sent them out of town." Winthrop, however, brought the sachem and the rest of his company to his house and "made much of them," as before, which seemed to please the party highly. Miantonomo was much incensed at the behavior of his attendants and ordered the offenders immediately to leave town. That same Sunday the chief also departed. On at least six other occasions did he appear before the authorities of Massachusetts Bay. He was continually requested or even ordered to come to Boston to reaffirm his friendliness to the colonists and directly he had departed the magistrates again became uneasy as to his attitude and Miantonomo would again have to follow the long Narragansett trail eastward. Although he assisted the English to defeat the warlike Pequots in 1637 he was still distrusted and his unfortunate end is described later in this chapter. On his visit to Boston on October 21, 1636 he made an agreement to assist the colonists. He brought with him two sons of Canonicus and a large retinue and was welcomed at Roxbury by twenty musketeers and escorted into Boston at noon. It is said that he was well received by Governor Vane, who entertained the Sachem and his council at his house, though not at the same table, as Governor Winthrop was wont to do, while his sannops were dined at Cole's Inn in Merchant's Row. On the following day articles of agreement were signed, and dinner was again served at the Governor's house, whereupon the Indians were escorted out of Boston by a corps of musketeers, who saluted them with a volley of shot. Roger Williams explained to them later the treaty they had already signed. In March of the following year, 1637, to show his faithfulness in warring against the Pequots, Miantonomo sent to Winthrop, who was again serving as governor, twenty-six of his men with the gruesome but quite customary present of a Pequot's hand, and forty fathom of wampum.

On November 1, 1637, Miantonomo made another official visit to Boston and was received again by Winthrop. On this occasion the Governor, deputy governor and treasurer "treated with him, and they parted upon fair terms," as the diary expresses it. Miantonomo acknowledged that all the Pequot country and Block Island belonged to the English and he promised not to interfere except by permission of the colonists. We do not hear of him again in Boston for three years. It was reported that he was endeavoring to be elected Sachem of all the near-by Indians and therefore Thomas Dudley, who served as Governor during the latter part of 1640, dispatched Captain Jenyson to the Narragansett Sachems toward the late summer to learn the truth of their intentions. Propaganda existed in those days, for one learns that the people of Plymouth had also heard rumors that Mian-

5

tonomo was endeavoring to persuade the Mohawks to help him against the English. The Wampanoags were doubtless busy circulating these false reports. Jenyson was well received, but as he had as an interpreter a Pequot, who was a servant and an enemy, they refused to discuss matters until another interpreter was called in. They denied any confederacy with the Mohawks, and Miantonomo promised to appear in Boston and answer to these charges, provided Roger Williams might go with him. This request was refused, but the Narragansett Sachem nevertheless appeared again in Boston on November 9th. At this time he was met at Dorchester by Captain Gibbons and a guard of twelve musketeers, and then entertained by Governor Thomas Dudley at his home in Roxbury on the site long occupied by the First Universalist Church, which was burned toward the close of the 19th century. Quite naturally the visitor refused to parley with the magistrates of the Bay Colony in the presence of the Pequot interpreter supplied by Dudley. "When your people come to me, they are permitted to use their own fashions," the Sachem declared, "and I expect the same liberty when I come to you." The Governor was just as determined, and refused to make use of any other interpreter, thinking, as Winthrop wrote, "it a dishonour to us to give so much way to them." "Whereupon," continues Winthrop, "he came from Roxbury to Boston, departing in a rude manner, without showing any respect or sign of thankfulness to the governour for his entertainment, whereof the governour informed the general court, and would show him no countenance, nor admit him to dine at our table, as formerly he had done, till he had acknowledged his failing, etc., which he readily did, so soon as he could be made to understand it, and did speak with our committees and us by a Pequot maid who could speak English perfectly." He had been obliged to give in to the wishes of his hosts, most of whom were under arms. The court nevertheless still believed he was withholding facts. Nothing was agreed to except that one article was added to the former articles of treaty, all of which were acknowledged by him. The late H. M. Chapin of the Rhode Island Historical Society states of this interview: "The unjust, arbitrary and overbearing insistence by the Massachusetts Bay authorities that Miantonomo converse through an interpreter who belonged to a tribe hostile to him, cannot be justified and might well have brought on a war, had not the Indians been far more peaceable, considerate and forgiving than the colonists."

Miantonomo must have spent a great deal of time in answering the summonses of Boston, Hartford and Providence, and the trails from his camps to these towns must have been very familiar to him. The Indians were accustomed to covering long distances in remarkably short time. It is amusing to compare their long journeys from camp to camp with the moves that our ancestors used to make when for the summer they changed their residences from Salem Street down town to the top of Beacon Hill so as to get the benefit of the cool air.

Miantonomo's next visit to our city was in September of the year 1642, when he came at the request of the authorities. Two days were spent by the court of Massachusetts in examining him, and concerning this interview we will quote Drake: "and we are astonished at the wisdom of the great chief, even as reported by his enemies. That a simple man of nature, who never knew courts or law, should cause such acknowledgments as follow, from the civilized and wise, will always be contemplated with intense admiration. 'When he came,' says Winthrop, 'the court was assembled, and before his admission, we considered how to treat with him, (for we knew him to be a very subtile man).' When he was admitted, 'he was set down at the lower end of the table, over against the governour,' but would not speak of any business at any time before some of his counsellors were present; saying 'he would have them present, that they might bear witness with him, at his return home, of all his sayings.'" The same author further says, "In all his answers he was very deliberate, and showed good understanding in the principles of justice and equity, and ingenuity withal."

"He now asked for his accusers, urging, that if they could not establish their allegations, they ought to suffer what he expected to, if they did; but the court said they knew of none; . . . he then said, 'If you did not give credit to it, why then did you disarm the Indians?' (Massachusetts had just then disarmed some of the Merrimacks under some pretence.) 'He gave divers reasons,' says Governor Winthrop, 'why we should hold him free of any such conspiracy, and why we should conceive it was a report raised by Onkus, etc., and therefore offered to meet Onkus, . . . and would prove to his face his treachery against the English, etc., and told us he would come to us at any time.' The punishment due to those who had raised the accusations bore heavily upon his breast, and 'he put it to our consideration what damage it had been to him, in that he was forced to keep his men at home, and not suffer them to go forth on hunting, etc., till he had given the English satisfaction.' Finally the court reported 'he did accommodate himself to us to our satisfaction' and he also condescended that if the Niantics wronged the English, he would leave them to the English to punish. When dinner was served by Governor Winthrop a separate table was provided for the Indians, and Miantonomo was asked to sit with his compatriots. This arrangement did not please the chieftain and, as Winthrop states, he 'would eat nothing, till the governour sent him meat from his table. So at night, and all the time he staid, he sat at the lower end of the magistrate's table. When he departed, we gave him and his counsellors coats and tobacco, and when he came to take his leave of the governour, and such of the magistrates as were present, he returned, and gave his hand to the governour again, saying, that was for the rest of the magistrates who were absent.' One would not expect such politeness from a sachem."

Miantonomo made still another visit to Boston in June, 1643, owing to a disagreement in regard to the lands of Shawomet, now Warwick, Rhode Island. Pomham and Socononoco were also involved, and both journeyed to Boston on June 22, 1643 and submitted themselves and their lands to the government of Massachusetts. Massachusetts Bay then laid claim to Shawomet, but requested Miantonomo to appear before the authorities to decide the ownership of these lands and to prove his claim of sovereignty over the other two sachems. He promptly appeared, and as Winthrop records, "being demanded in open court, before divers of his own men and Cutshamekin and other

Indians, whether he had any interest in the said two sachems as his subjects, he could prove none." Governor Winthrop considered the submission of Pomham and Socononoco "as a fruit of our prayers, and the first fruit of our hopes, that the example would bring in others." They dined "in the same room with the governour, but at a table by themselves," according to this same record.

Between this visit in June and his death in August, Miantonomo made his seventh and last visit to Boston, while Winthrop was governor. It is probable that the governor had just moved from State Street to his new residence in Washington Street near the site of Old South Church, opposite the foot of School Street. His garden was situated on the present site of this Church. Uncas, Sachem of the Mohegans, claimed he had been wounded by a Pequot warrior, who had become a subject of his after the defeat of the Pequots by the English. When questioned, this Pequot fled to the Narragansetts. Uncas reported the incident to the Massachusetts authorities, charging that Miantonomo had attempted to kill him. To absolve himself the Narragansett Sachem journeyed to Boston with the Pequot, and denied any knowledge of the affair. The Pequot explained that Uncas had inflicted the wound on his own arm in order to implicate Miantonomo. The latter agreed to hand the supposed slayer over to Uncas, but instead of so doing he killed him soon after leaving Boston. A short time afterwards Miantonomo was captured by Uncas, and was assassinated by the latter at the instigation of the Court of Commissioners of the United Colonies of New England held at Boston.

Another famous Sachem to visit the leading town in Massachusetts was an uncle or a cousin of Miantonomo named Ninigret, also called Ninicraft, "King" of the Niantics of Westerly and later of Charlestown in Rhode Island. He is called by Mather "an old crafty sachem." He is known to have passed over the long trail on a number of occasions. His first call on Governor Winthrop was on July 12, 1637, when he came to Boston with seventeen men, making "divers propositions." The objects of his visit were stated, and an answer promised on the following day. The governor heard somehow in the meanwhile that Ninigret had harbored many Pequots after their defeat by the colonists at Mystic, and therefore refused to give any reply until the sachem promised first to deliver them up. Ninigret, who was referred to as Ayanemo in Winthrop's Journal, at first refused this demand, but the "next morning he came, and offered what we desired." The governor instructed him to treat with the English captains then in the Pequot country and after receiving from the visitor the customary present of wampum, "he was lovingly dismissed, with some small things given him," as the same journal expresses it. Some years later, on August 3, 1647, the Commissioners record that Ninigret with some of his Niantic Indians and two of Pessacus' men came to Boston and inquired for John Winthrop, who was still governor. There is a tradition that Ninigret saved the life of John Winthrop, Jr., a story that is given greater credence by the fact that a descendant of this early colonist has a portrait of this Sachem which is reproduced herewith, through the kindness of the late Frederic Winthrop of Boston. This Sachem "had professed his desire to be reconciled to the English," and also desired to complain of the behavior of Uncas. There was a considerable fracas over the promised payment of wampum and kettles which seems too complicated to discuss here. Ninigret bestowed a present on the governor and it now became also a question as to whether this was part of the debt. He therefore stated, "My tongue shall not belie my heart. Whether the debt be paid or not, I intended it as a present to the governor." This Niantic chief promised to raise the necessary wampum and dispatched some of his men to collect it, he himself remaining in Boston. Only a small part of the debt was procured and so the Commissioners finally allowed Ninigret to depart, but at the end of two years he had been no more successful than his messengers. In the meantime further complaints were received by the colonists from Uncas to the effect that the Narragansetts were seeking his ruin. At this time, during the year 1649, the English learned that Ninigret's daughter was to be married to the son of Sassacus' brother and feared therefore a union of tribes against them. Ninigret was summoned to Boston

Photographed from the original painting   *Kindness of the late Frederic Winthrop*

NINIGRET, FAMOUS SACHEM OF THE NIANTICS, A TRIBE OF THE NARRAGANSETTS, HAILING FROM WESTERLY AND LATER CHARLESTOWN, RHODE ISLAND

He was an uncle or cousin of Miantonomo. He visited Boston in July, 1637, as recorded by Governor Winthrop, and again in 1647 and 1649. This photograph is taken from an old original painting which has been in the Winthrop family for many years, and which is now owned by Grenville L. Winthrop of New York. There is a tradition that Ninigret once saved the life of a member of the family. This picture is said to be one of the very few authentic likenesses of an Indian chief that has come down to us.

and discussed the question with the Commissioners.

In 1668 Ninigret, with Pessacus and the Squaw Sachem, Magnus, were summoned to answer charges concerning certain land deals, and they again appeared with Moosup before the Governor's Council on August 27 and August 28 of the following year in connection with Indian disturbances. On several occasions he sent representatives to Boston, Awashaw coming at one time, and in September, 1675, eight of his men came as ambassadors. A few days later the authorities in Boston sent an order for Ninigret to appear himself to answer to the charge of sheltering Weetamoe, the Squaw Sachem of Pocasset. His son, however, decided to make the journey in place of his father, who was now old and too feeble to make the attempt. It is said that this delegation from Narragansett met a company of English soldiers at Roxbury and became so frightened at their warlike appearance that they were about to turn and run had not a friend, Captain Smith, who made the trip with them, allayed their fears. The visitors remained in Boston several days and finally came to an agreement which was never acknowledged, however, by Ninigret himself. Roger Williams mentions this chieftain in one of his letters, stating on his departure for England, "I was importuned by the Narragansett Sachems, and especially by Ninigret, to present their petition to the high Sachems of England, that they might not be forced from their religion, and for not changing their religion, to be invaded by war: for they said they were daily visited with threatenings by Indians that came from about the Massachusetts, that if they would not pray, they should be destroyed by war." On another occasion when Mayhew asked permission to preach among Ninigret's people, the Sachem replied, "Make the English good first, try it on the Pequots and Mohegans and if it works, I will consider it." At another time when he was urged to adopt Christianity, he replied that "as long as the English could not agree as to which was religion, among themselves, it ill became them to teach others."

Another important Indian to visit Governor Winthrop was Uncas, a King of the Mohegans, who is buried in the Royal Burying-ground of that tribe in Norwich, Connecticut. Uncas left his Pequot tribe, of which he was a captain, and set up as Sachem of the Mohegans about the year 1634. Although deceitful and treacherous, he became nevertheless a fast friend of the English, who he doubtless believed would assist him in warding off his enemies on the North and South. In the late spring of the year 1638, he came to Governor Winthrop, the only visit he made to Boston during his long life, as far as can be learned. The same journal thus describes this event:

"Unkus, alias Okoco, the Monahegan sachem in the twist of Pequod River, came to Boston with thirty-seven men. He came from Connecticut with Mr. Haynes, and tendered the governour a present of twenty fathoms of wampom. This was at the court, and it was thought fit by the council to refuse it, till he had given satisfaction about the Pequods he kept, etc. Upon this he was much dejected, and made account we would have killed him; but, two days after, having received good satisfaction of his innocency, etc., and he promising to submit to the order of the English touching the Pequods he had, and the differences between the Narragansetts and him, we accepted his present. And, about half an hour after, he came to the governour, and entertained him with these compliments: 'This heart (laying his hand upon his breast) is not mine, but yours; I have no men; they are all yours; command me any difficult thing, I will do it; I will not believe any Indians' words against the English; if any man shall kill an Englishman, I will put him to death, were he never so dear to me.' So the governour gave him a fair, red coat, and defrayed his and his men's diet, and gave them corn to relieve them homeward, and a letter of protection to all men, etc., and he departed very joyful."

The great and life-long friend of the Pilgrims of course was Massasoit. He came to Boston twice from one of his three seats in the Wampanoag Country; Sowams, now Bristol, Rhode Island; Middleborough, Massachusetts; or from his summer camp near Fowling Pond in Raynham, also in Massachusetts. The first visit of which we have any record is described by Winthrop who was serving as Governor. "Ousamekin, (another name for Massasoit and meaning Yellow-Feather) the sachem of Acooemeck, on this side Connecticut, came to the governour and brought a present of eighteen skins of beaver from himself and the sachems of Mohegan beyond Connecticut and Pakontuckett. The occasion was, (as he said,) it was reported, that we were angry with him, and intended to war upon them; so they came to seek peace. The governour received the present, and (having none of the other magistrates at hand to advise with) answered them, that if they had done no wrong to the English, nor aided our enemies, we would be at peace with them; and accordingly signified so much to the magistrates at Connecticut. They took this answer well, and departed with the letter." The date was April 21, 1638. Four years later he again journeyed to our city and this brief notice appears in Winthrop's Diary under date of July 21: "Osamaken, the great sachem of Pakanocott in Plymouth jurisdiction, came, attended with many men and some other sagamores accompanying him, to visit the governour, who entertained him kindly, etc." Even Winthrop's ways of spelling this Sachem's name seem to have varied.

We have spoken of Chickatabot who had his chief seat at Squantum. He was succeeded by his brother-in-law Cutshamakin who resided at Neponset Mill, now Dorchester Lower Mills. While leader of the Massachusetts tribe he sold Unquity, now part of Milton, to the people of Dorchester in 1636. That same year Massachusetts sent this sachem to Block Island as interpreter with some English to inquire of the Pequots concerning the recent murder of John Oldham. This Indian captured one of the Pequots, then shot and scalped him, causing Captain Leon Gardener to write: "I had written in a book, that all men and posterity might know how and why so many honest men had their blood shed, yea, and some flayed alive, others cut in pieces, and some roasted alive, only because Kichamokin, a Bay Indian, killed one Pequot." In the summer of this same year this Massachusetts Sachem, with Lieutenant Edward Gibbons and Rev. John Higginson, left Boston on another expedition, this time to the Court of Canonicus at Narragansett. Edward Johnson in his "Wonder-Working

Providence of Sion's Saviour" gives such a realistic account of their reception by the royal court that we quote the lines selected by Mr. Chapin: "The Indian King, hearing of their coming, gathered together his chief counsellors, and a great number of his subjects to give them entertainment, . . . were entertained royally with respect to the Indian manner. Boiled chestnuts is their white bread, which are very sweet, as if they were mixed with sugar, and because they would be extraordinary in their feasting, they strive for vanity after the English manner, boiled puddings made of beaten corn, putting therein great store of black berries, somewhat like currants. They having thus nobly feasted them, afterwards gave them

Photographed from an old print   *Kindness of Chester H. Phillips*
MEETING OF GOVERNOR CARVER AND MASSASOIT

audience in a State House. . . . In this place sat their Sachem, with very great attendance; . . . the Indian sachem lay along the ground on a mat and his nobility sat on the ground with their legs doubled up, their knees touching their chins, . . . It was a matter of much wonderment to the English to see how solidly and wisely these savage people did consider of the weighty undertaking of a war, . . ."

In September, six years later, the colonists sent some of their men to Braintree, where Cutshamakin had another camp, to bring him and his weapons to Boston. They evidently had become suspicious of him, for we read that although he came willingly, he was at once put into prison. Upon examination the next morning he and his men were freed, as no ground was discovered for suspicion of his partaking in any conspiracy. He was thereupon dismissed.

In February, 1644, Cutshamakin, Agawam and Josias Chickatabot, son of the well-known Indian already often referred to, gave Governor Winthrop a present of the customary wampum or Indian money and offered to appear before the next court and make their acknowledgment of submission. The Governor was careful to keep the present until the court and the Indians came to an agreement, which did not come about until the next March. According to their promise the following Indians put in an appearance a short time later: Cutshamakin; Squaw Sachem, Widow of Nanepashmet; Masconomo of Ipswich, already spoken of; Nashacowam and Wassamagin, the latter two hailing from "the great hill" to the west called Wachusett. They were received on the same terms as Pomham and Socononoco and were to receive the same protection as the English subjects themselves. The Boston Puritans asked Cutshamakin to have his people refrain from unnecessary work on Sundays, to which he is said to have replied that this arrangement suited him as they didn't have much to do on any day. The diary contains this further entry, "And the court gave each of them a coat of two yards of cloth, and their dinner; and to them and their men every one of them a cup of sack at their departure, so they took leave and went away very joyful." "We now began to conceive hope," wrote Winthrop, "that the Lord's time was at hand for opening a door of light and grace to those Indians, and some fruit appeared of our kind dealing with Pomham and Socononoco, protecting them against the Narragansett, and righting them against Gorton, etc., who had taken away their land: for this example gave encouragement to all these Indians to come in and submit to our government, in expectation of the like protection and benefit." Cutshamakin signed treaties with the Boston magistrates in 1643 and again in the summer of 1645. Although at first he was unfriendly, he later served them in many ways and was finally christianized. To him and his Indians John Eliot first preached in his wigwam at Dorchester Mills in the year 1647.

A few days after Cutshamakin's submission to the English at Boston in 1644, Pessacus who had just assumed, at the age of twenty, the leadership of the Narragansetts after the death of his brother Miantonomo a short time before, sent a present to Winthrop by an Indian called Washose with the request that as they "had sitten still this year," that now they be permitted to fight against Uncas for the murder of his brother Miantonomo. "The Governour refused his present, and told him that if they sent us 1000 fathom of wampom and 1000 skins, yet we would not do that which we judged to be unjust, viz. to desert Onkus." In October of the previous year he had sent fifteen pounds of Indian money stating that he desired peace and friendship and begged the English not to assist Uncas against him. Winthrop sent the answer that "We desire withal that there might be peace with all Indians also."

While Thomas Dudley was Governor, Pessacus, Mixanno, the eldest son of Canonicus and others visited Boston and negotiated a treaty in 1645.

Governor Dudley also received messengers from Sassacus, Chief of the warlike Pequots, whose name was a terror to the Indian tribes near by. On November 9, 1634, a treaty was entered into at Boston whereby that tribe agreed to deliver up to the English the murderers of Captain Stone, who had recently been killed while on a trading expedition to the Connecticut River. During the month previous he had sent a messenger upon the same errand, who was ordered to return and to send persons of greater rank before consideration would be given. This Indian representative "brought two bundles of sticks," explains Winthrop, "whereby he signified how many beaver and otter skins he would give us for that end, and great store of wampomeage." The Governor presented him with a "moose coat of as good value." The colonists were going through a critical period of their history and were never sure they would not be attacked by the Pequots. Then followed the war which practically wiped out that tribe. On August 5, 1637, anxiety was further dispelled, as Governor Winthrop wrote under this date that "Mr. Ludlow, Mr. Pincheon and about twelve more, came the ordinary way by land, and brought with them a part of the skin and lock of hair of Sasacus and his brother . . ." and so while Sassacus never visited Boston the colonists at least had this satisfaction, which to us seems gruesome, but meant perhaps life and death to them.

Miantonomo's son called Canonchet and later known as Nanunteno, one of the bravest of men, inherited the chief sachemdom of the Narragansetts. In 1674 he was elected "chief surviving sachem" of that tribe and on October 18 of the following year, just before King Philip's war broke out, he visited Boston. John Leverett, who was baptised in St. Botolph's Church in Boston, England, was the Governor at that time. The chieftain signed on this visit a treaty confirming an old one. He was presented with a coat trimmed with silver. His name stands first in this treaty, in which he called himself Quananchett.

King Philip himself journeyed to Boston in the autumn of 1671, a few months after the Taunton Treaty. Secretary Morton of the Plymouth Colony sent word to the Massachusetts authorities that they would "send forces to reduce him to reason" unless he complied with that treaty and handed over more of their guns. Philip immediately repaired to Boston and appealed to our magistrates against these demands from Plymouth. He informed the authorities that his father had signed with the Plymouth colony treaties of amity and not of subjection. He insisted that he was a subject of the King of England, but not a subject of any of his colonies. The authorities in Massachusetts urged the magistrates of Plymouth to avoid a conflict if possible.

The records of the Colony of New Plymouth contain this paragraph in regard to this incident: "On the 13th of September, 1671, the councell of warr appeered according to theire sumons, but Phillip, the sachem, appeered not, but in sted therof repaired to the Massachusetts, and made complaint against vs to diuers of the gentlemen in place there, whoe wrote to our Gour by way of pswasion, to aduise the Councell to a complyance with the said sachem."

Philip appeared in Plymouth on two or three occasions. It is said that after his death his two hands were sent to Boston as trophies of victory.

NANTUCKET AND THE INDIAN

When a tradition has been handed down from generation to generation, it often becomes accepted as established fact. In the case we are about to mention, a visit made in 1665 to the island by the famous King Philip, Metacomet, a long-standing tradition is backed up by four well-known authorities on Nantucket history — Henry B. Worth, Douglas-Lithgow, and Zaccheus and Obed Macy, the latter two both descendants of one of the original settlers of the island. Obed Macy's memory would go well back into the 17th century, and he stated that the story was handed down to him by his ancestors and that he did not doubt the truth of it. Samuel G. Drake, however, considers it still a matter of tradition. No definite proof has ever been found, but if the original Indian inhabitants succeeded in canoeing from Cape Cod or the Vineyard to Nantucket, it would have been equally possible for Philip and his band of warriors to accomplish this same feat.

In some way the intruder King Philip heard that Assassamoogh, familiarly known as John Gibbs, in violation of sacred Indian custom, had profaned the name of a dead Indian, supposedly King Philip's father, Massasoit, and Philip determined therefore to wreak vengeance upon the culprit, the usual punishment for this crime being death. The story seems to vary, but Philip and his sizable army are supposed to have landed on the west end of the island and then to have proceeded along the shore under the bank so as not to be detected. Their presence was discovered by an Indian who succeeded in warning the intended victim of their approach. Assassamoogh fled into the English settlement to the house of Thomas Macy, the original settler. We will let Obed Macy give his version of what ensued: "There being but a small number of English at that time, they had everything to fear. Philip's hostile appearance and preparations made them apprehensive that he would destroy them if any measures were taken to arrest his progress in pursuit of the delinquent. On the other hand, if they assisted to search after him, they dreaded the revenge of the island natives. They therefore declined lending their aid in any respect. Philip then went with his party in pursuit of the criminal, and at length found him on the south-east part of the island. . . . Philip, having now the poor criminal in possession, made preparations to execute vengeance upon him, when the English spectators commiserated his condition and made offers of money to ransom his life. Philip listened to these offers and mentioned a sum which would satisfy him; but so much could not be collected. He was informed of this, but refused to lessen his demand. The whites, however, collected all they could in the short time allowed them, in hopes that he would be satisfied. . . . The sum raised, which was all the inhabitants possessed, was eleven pounds; this had already been paid to him, and could not be required back again. Philip had surrounded and taken possession of one or two houses, to the great terror of the inmates; in this dilemma they concluded to put all to risk; they told him, that, if he did not immediately leave the island, they would rally the inhabitants, and fall upon him and cut him off to a man. Not knowing their defenceless condition, he happily took the alarm and left the island as soon as possible. The prisoner was then set at liberty."

Drake asserts that Gibbs escaped his pursuer by running from house to house and then by jumping down a high bank. A swamp through which the two are supposed to have raced is still known as Philip's Run. It is well that Gibbs' life was spared, for he later became converted to Christianity by Thomas Mayhew, and then preached to the Nantucket and Vineyard Indians for many years. His name is still attached to the pond near the 'Sconset Road, about five miles from Nantucket Village, for here at Oggawame or Okawaw, near Plainfield, was situated the largest of the Indian villages on the island, where he resided and near by was the Indian Church over which he presided.

Obed Macy, Douglas-Lithgow and Alexander Starbuck are again authorities for the statement that Metacomet, King Philip, tried in vain to induce the Nantucket Indians to join him in his war against the English. They replied in his presence that they were entirely satisfied and wished to remain at peace with the whites. Douglas-Lithgow quotes a record from the town meeting held on the island on October 10, 1665, but upon inquiry it was learned that there are now no town records in existence as early as that year, although there may have been at some time. A leading Nantucket authority reaffirms the statement that the early records kept by Peter Folger completely disappeared, and adds that the visit of King Philip "is not alluded to in the Town Records and seems to be a matter of tradition, but there seem to be some corroboratory circumstances which make it entirely probable. . . . It is not unlikely that the friendly act of Attaychat declaring allegiance of himself and his people to the English King as shown by the Town Records in October of that year was attributable to this intervention of the English against Philip." The actual wording of this interesting record is as follows: "When King Philip visited the island in 1665 and tried to induce the natives to join in his contemplated war with the English, they emphatically refused to do so, expressing themselves as perfectly satisfied and desiring to be at peace with the whites." Douglas-Lithgow states that at a town meeting on October 10, 1665, Attaychat (Autopscott) "signified that himself with all the Tomokommoth Indians subject to the English Government in Nantucket acknowledge subjection to King Charles II. This was done in the presence of Metacomet, alias Philip, Sachem of Mount Hope." Starbuck's version of this record is somewhat different: "October 10th, 1665. At a publick Meeting of the Town Attaychat signified that himself with all the Tomokommoth Indians doth subject to the English Government of Nantucket, do owne themselves subjects to King Charles the Second — this was don in the presence of Molocon, alias Philip Sachem of Mount Hope." It would seem as if this must be an accurate copy of some record, and probably it is the most authentic proof of Philip's hurried visit. He is reported to have returned to his seat at Mount Hope in Bristol rather chagrined over the fact that his only prize was the eleven pounds presented to him by the English to bribe him to depart.

We will not dwell upon the two tribes of Indians that settled on the island, one at the east end and the other in the western part, with their various bickerings and romances. The former tribe is supposed to have reached its destination from across the Sound, and the latter coming by way of Martha's Vineyard, though remaining still as subjects of the Wampanoags. Nor will we attempt to describe their occasional battles, the territory occupied, their Christian Churches established at a later period, their cemeteries, or their leading sachems. We will also pass over the arrival of the first white settlers led by Thomas Macy and the many early deeds to the acquired lands, some of which are still in existence. The second purchase included the whole island and the price paid is well known, for the seller insisted on receiving not only thirty pounds, but, as he amusingly expressed it, "also two Beaver Hatts, one for myself and one for my Wife." The earliest Indian deed in existence is dated June 20, 1659, but was not recorded until 1731.

In speaking of Nantucket it is always interesting to remember that Peter Folger, born in Norwich, England, was asked to remove from the Vineyard to Nantucket to act as interpreter for the early settlers. He was evidently a man of all trades, for we read of his acting also as miller, weaver, surveyor of lands, blacksmith, keeper of the records, preacher, schoolmaster and author. There could have been little for anyone else to do. His chief accomplishment, however, was the fact that he became the grandfather of Benjamin Franklin, his daughter Abiah having married Josiah Franklin.

We think it may be of interest to enumerate some Indian customs of the early days, as well as some of their most curious laws, regulations and court procedures connected with the island history. Nantucketers always referred to a picnic to be held at no definite place as a "vantum scool," and if the location had been selected it was called a "squantum" after the place of the same name near Boston. At one of these parties one of those present when asked if he would have another helping is said to have replied, "Well, don't mind if I do, for I've come with my 'squantum' vest on," meaning that on such occasions he wore an extra spacious waistcoat, so that he might "cater to his taste without restraint." The Indians on the island had a curious custom of punishing their children. They steeped some bayberry root in water and taking the mixture into their mouths they would squirt it into the noses of the children. This method of punishment, called by them "Medomhumar," it is claimed, produced very quickly the desired results.

Many laws were passed to regulate the conduct of the aborigines, and a few may be worth while enumerating. The question of horses and goats was an important one, as they were increasing rapidly and pasturage was limited. At an early town meeting it was declared

that, "Horses are like to be the ruine of our neat cattel and the multitude of goats is very hurtful." It was decided therefore that some-
thing must be done "about cleering the yland," and a vote was
passed "that all horses shall be taken off the yland or be destroyed
before the last of November." The dogs destroyed the crops and it
was decided to pass some regulations concerning them, therefore it
was proclaimed that "All Indians are to kill all their dogs, and if any
dogs be found alive after ten days the owner shall pay to the English
two shillings for every one." The Indians were very fond of their
pets and paid little attention to these rulings, therefore it was found
necessary to pass another law, placing a time limit for the destruction of the animals; and to ensure the carrying out of this statute
two Englishmen and two Indians were empowered to collect the
fines. "Fire-water" caused the Indians to commit crimes and mis-
demeanors, whereupon the English decided it best to appoint a
prominent Indian to act as a superintendent or local magistrate. The
first person so chosen was James Shouel, known also as Korduda,
and he managed his compatriots with an iron hand. It is said that he
always gave orders to have both the complainant and the defendant
severely whipped, a procedure which usually proved effective. This
original method of handling cases was known as "Korduda's law."
Sometimes the English and the Indians were called upon to work
together for the common good, as in the case of digging a "trench to
drean the Long pond forthwith with regard to a ware (weir) for
taking fish."

At one time there was on the island an Indian Court, although its
decisions could be reviewed by the English. The existence of this
native tribunal was learned from the appeals that were made to the
English Court. An Indian was accused before the latter body of
resisting the authority of the Indian Court by reviling speeches and a
paddle. He testified that their magistrates were unjust, and in several
cases this was learned to be so and the opinions handed down were
reversed. There is evidence that the Indians also had their justices,
constables and grand jury men, and the names of a few of those who
served in these positions have been handed down to us. Some of the
decisions indicate the difficulties that arose between the two races. A
few of the most curious of these court records we will enumerate. On
March 25, 1679, one Coffin complained against an Indian "for lying
and other rude carages," and the "sentance" imposed by the Court
was that "this Endian shall set toe (two) ours in the Stocks next
trayning day." An Indian woman was fined on account of "being
Inditted for Telling severall lyes." Branding was the usual punishment inflicted upon an aborigine for stealing. When an Indian had
no money, corn, oil or feathers he sometimes pledged his canoe, as in
the case of Aspatchamo, who "delivereth his Canoe unto William
Worth for secuerity for his fine." When unable to deliver anything
of any value it was customary to force the culprit into the service of
the English or even to serve their own Sachems, which in either case
was practically slavery. In this way John Macy obtained for three
years an Indian who was convicted of stealing sheep. Nathaniel
Starbuck and Peter Coffin had an Indian given them for a much
longer period of time for making off with "three payles of strong beer

17

one Galon of molases, two galons of Rum," which belonged to them. As William Bliss points out in his "Quaint Nantucket," the easy way to secure a house servant was to catch an Indian in the act of stealing. Evidently there were many attempts to escape from this form of slavery, and perhaps some were successful, for as early as the year 1670 a law was passed fining any Englishman or Indian who shall "carry away from the island without a permit any Indian servant."

There are also some Court records concerning domestic matters, a few of which we will mention. As early as 1677, a redskin named Quench applied for a "disvourse," which was granted, and his wife was at the same time fined twenty shillings "in Regard to his trobell." Another native husband who "put away his wife" was ordered to take her back and "live loveingly with her or else he shall be severely punished." Occasionally a breach of promise case was brought before the Court, usually punishable by whipping, and one record shows that an Indian woman complained of a certain man at the "non performance of his covenant with her he having Promised her marrag, and the sd John owned he had done soe." The Court ruled that "if John doe not marry the Squaw he shal be whipt twenty strips and pay the woman thirty shillings." Sometimes divorce seems to have been granted rather easily in Nantucket, for the Court once issued a proclamation ordering the public crier to proceed through the streets announcing that "If the Nanespepo wife return not unto her husband within six weeks after ye day, Nanespepo is free from her."

The connection that the red men have had with the whaling industry is one of the most interesting and least known subjects concerning the island's history. It is a well established fact that they were skillful whalemen in their way before the arrival of the white settlers. The earliest authority seems to have been George Weymouth, who visited our shores as early as 1605 and reported: "One especial thing in their manner of killing a whale which they (the Indians) call powdawe, and will describe his form, how he bloweth up the water, and that he is twelve fathoms long, and that they go in company with their King, with a multitude of their boats, and strike him with a bone made in the fashion of a harping iron, fastened to a rope, which they make great and strong of the bark of trees which they veer out after him; that all their boats come about him, and as he riseth above water, with their arrows they shoot him to death. When they have killed him and dragged him to shore, they call all their chief lords together, and sing a song of joy, and these chief lords, whom they call sagamores, divide the spoil and give to every man a share; which pieces so distributed they hang up about their houses for provision, and when they boil them they blow off the fat, and put in their pease, maize, and other pulse which they eat." Another much later visitor, St. John de Crevecœur, tells us that "In this business many Indians were employed, each boat's crew being manned in part, some wholly, by aborigines, the most active among them being promoted to steersmen, and even at times one of them being allowed to command a boat. Under the stimulus of this encouragement they soon became experienced whalemen and conversant with all the details of the business. . . . Their skill and dexterity in all sea affairs is nothing inferior to that of the whites." He also said it "often happened that whaling vessels were manned with none but Indians and the master." We doubt, however, if this was often so. Some of the Indians even reached the distinction of being able to wear a "Y" peg in their button-holes. These pegs were inserted in a wooden "Y" at the bow of the boat, through which the harpoon lines passed, and only a harpooner could wear this distinguished badge of honor. It is said jokingly that a harpooner was as proud of his first whale as an Indian was of his first scalp. The boys of the island were naturally brought up in an atmosphere of whaling talk, and occasionally a little tot, as soon as he could talk, would use the word "Tounor," meaning in the Indian language, "I have twice seen the whale." Another expression used by the Indian whalers was "Awarte Pawana," meaning "Here is a whale." It is related in Nantucket that a baby whale once followed an ocean liner into the harbor of New York, believing the liner was its mother.

Spears in his "Story of the New England Whalers" states that "the first white men to explore the coast of New England found red whalers at work. In every clan and tribe along the coast were men accustomed to killing whales." He adds that "Most interesting to the humanitarian is every record of things done by the red men of America in the days when they were undefiled by contact with the white race. And of the stories of the things done, few if any portray red manhood in brighter colors than those relating to the whale fishery." We must remember not only were their stone-headed spears very crude, but they had to put to sea, often in the winter, in their frail canoes. "What they lacked in implements," writes the same author, "they made up with courage, ingenuity and perseverance." Another writer says: "There is no doubt that the Natick (Massachusetts) Indians hunted the whale in canoes, in a manner somewhat similar to that practised today by the Bow-Headers of the north coast of Siberia." Douglas-Lithgow is another authority for the statement that "hunting the whale was well-known and long practised by the Nantucket Indians. . . . There can be no doubt that they joined gladly in the chase and that they were fully as dexterous as the whites not only in securing, but in dealing with the carcasses afterwards."

Soon after the whites arrived they began to instruct the Indians in their method of fishing, and in return the newcomers were helped by the Indians in the pursuit of this industry. As the two races were together a good deal of the time, each learned the other's language, a fact that made the Indian more and more valuable and useful to the English. Different sinkers and hooks were introduced. When the English took up whaling, the Indians, as made clear by Obed Macy, "ever manifesting a disposition for fishing of every kind, readily joined with the whites in this new pursuit, and willingly submitted to any station assigned them. By their assistance, the whites were enabled to fit out and man a far greater number of boats than they could have done of themselves. Nearly every boat was manned in part, many almost entirely, by natives; some of the most active of them were made steersmen, and some were allowed even to head the boats; thus encouraged, they soon became experienced whalemen, and capable of conducting any part of the business." Spears claims that more than one American whale-ship has had Indians for mates, but there is no record of anyone ever having risen to the position of Captain. The same writer says that "It is not unlikely that the first whale boat that was set afloat by the white settlers was manned in part by Indians, and in all times until the present day red men and white have been found pulling together to the tune of 'a dead whale or a stove boat.' The records say that they have always been good oarsmen and the very best of harpoon throwers." The expeditions were at first of short duration. Starbuck explains that "Indians were usually employed by the English, the whites furnishing all the necessary implements, and the Indians receiving a stipulated proportion of oil in payment." The Indians soon became dexterous in the use of the white men's implements, and moreover proved themselves profitable for the reason that they accepted as payment the most undesirable portions of the whale. In fact, they were so important to the whaling industry that during the uprisings between the colonists and the Indians in 1724 and 1725, the friendly Indians from Cape Cod, by previous agreement, were discharged in time to take part in the fall and winter whale-fishery. It was undoubtedly the same with regard to any of the Nantucket Indians who may have been in service of the whites. It is a curious thing that the names of none of the Indians who took part in the whaling industry have ever come down to us, with the exception of any Indian names that may occur in log books of the voyages.

Of course there were innumerable rows between the two races over the disposition of the whales, and laws had to be passed to take care of any situations that might arise. The first sperm whale known to Nantucket was found stranded on the southwest part of the island. There was naturally much excitement, and numbers of persons who viewed the strange creature claimed part of the prize under some pretext or other. The remainder of the story is better told by Starbuck: "There were so many claimants of the prize," he said, "that it was difficult to determine to whom it should belong. The natives claimed the whale because they found it (not a bad reason surely); the whites, to whom the natives made known their discovery, claimed it by a right comprehended, as they affirmed, in the purchase of the island. (Ah! what lawyers they must have been!) An officer of the crown (here steps in the lion) made his claim, and pretended to seize the fish in the name of His Majesty, as being property without any particular owner. . . . It was finally settled that the white inhabitants who first found the whale, should share the prize equally amongst themselves. (Alas for royalty, and alas for the finders!) The teeth, considered very valuable, had been prudently taken care of by a white man and an Indian before the discovery was made public." The result was that a number of laws were passed. In the early deeds of some of our towns the Indian grantors were permitted to keep the fins and tails of all drift whales. Later it was found advisable to divide the shares into sections. The town of Southampton on Long Island was more generous and voted that the whites and Indians should divide the whale equally. Another of the town's votes read "That whosoever shall Hire an Indyan to go a-Whaling, shall not give him for his Hire above one Trucking Cloath Coat, for each whale, hee and his Company shall Kill, or halfe the

Blubber, without the Whale Bone. . . ." There also was another regulation that any agreements between the two races in regard to the killing of whales should be entered upon the town books and that every man must take his turn in watching for whales.

There were many Court decisions with respect to stranded whales, and many references too numerous to mention appear in the Registry of Deeds.

There are a few whaling stories that have not gone the rounds as much as some others and might stand repetition. An old whaleman with his bread in one hand and his knife in the other requested one of his family to "Put that butter within darting distance, please."

Another story is told of a boy of nine who tied one end of his mother's ball of darning cotton to a fork and tried to harpoon the family pet cat as it was about to "sound" through the window.

Zaccheus Macy tells of an incident that happened in the early days when whaling was carried on in small boats along the outer shore. "It happened once, when there were about thirty boats about six miles from the shore, that the wind came round to the northward, and blew with great violence, attended with snow. The men all rowed hard, but made but little headway. In one of the boats there were four Indians and two white men. An old Indian in the head of the boat, perceiving that the crew began to be disheartened, spake out loud in his own tongue and said, 'Momadickchator auqua sarshkee sarnkee pinchee eynoo sememoochkee chaquanks wihchee pinchee eynoo'; which in English is, 'Pull ahead with courage: do not be disheartened: we shall not be lost now: there are too many Englishmen to be lost now.' His speaking in this manner gave the crew new courage. They soon perceived that they made headway; and after long rowing, they all got safe on shore."

There are a number of other stories flavored with the customary Nantucket salt, collected in the "Nantucket Scrap Basket," by William F. Macy, which are used by permission of the publishers, Houghton Mifflin Co. It is said that a Quaker minister, seeing that a good many of his congregation were occupying the back seats, leaving the front ones comparatively empty, started his discourse by remarking, "Come, fleet for'ard, friends; there's too much weight aft." While attending an oyster stew supper at a church, one of those present is said to have made this remark to the waitress, "See here, my lassie, can't ye get me some more oysters? These here are a day's sail apart." Once a Nantucket mother was heard to tell her children to "splice their patience," and at another time when she had to go out on an errand she informed one of the older ones in the family please to "tend the kitchen halyards," until she returned. When the whaling industry was on the decline and fewer whalers were being sent out, the head of the house would occasionally rebuke his "better half" for extravagance with the amusing remark "Two lamps burning and no ship at sea." Macy also tells of a sailor who had had about all the sea he wanted. He told a friend he had decided to "shoulder an oar and march inland till somebody asked him what that thing was he was carrying, and there he would settle for the rest of his days." One time two Nantucketers chanced to meet and during their conversation one asked the other how he was able during these hard times to feed his large family on his small income. "Well, I'll tell you," came the reply. "I find out what they don't like and give them plenty of it." Several ship captains were swapping ideas over the dinner table one evening and one of them "got off" these few lines:

> "If navigating through this life
>   In poverty or riches,
> You chance to meet a head-on sea
>   Just ease her where she pitches."

We have heard of the Nantucket captain who was so familiar with the soundings around the island that upon tasting the lead which his mate had, as a joke on the captain, dipped in the earth from a box of parsnips on deck, he informed his crew that he believed Nantucket had sunk and that they were right over "Ma'am Hackett's" garden. Macy also tells us of Captain Baxter who was able to take his soundings on land on a dark night. While driving some friends across the Commons to 'Sconset he was seen occasionally to hit the road with the handle of his whip and then to taste the dust that came up with it. His companions asked him why he continued to repeat this performance, and he replied, "Why, bless you, I know this old island blindfolded the darkest night that ever was. I just take a sounding, and I can tell to a foot where we are by the taste of the bottom." We have also heard of a government official who once referred to the Swiss Navy, but the writer of this amusing "Scrap Basket" of stories reminds his readers about a lost car tracer on a Western Railroad who telegraphed the superintendent of the now obsolete Nantucket Railroad asking him if a certain freight car of his had by chance got side-tracked onto the Nantucket road.

The record of the Nantucket Indians during the various wars was an excellent one. Many precautions, nevertheless, were taken to ensure their amity. Governor Andros sent to the island "a couple of great Guns and halfe a Dousen Soulders." A Council of War was formed and rules were passed affecting the Indians. Among these was a regulation that no person was allowed to furnish powder or shot or to sell a horse to an Indian. None of these precautionary measures were necessary, as the redskins showed no animosity whatever; in fact, as we have mentioned, not only did they submit to the King and hand over their guns, but they disowned one of their number; and one of them, in order to be sure to be on the right side, in regard to doing what was proper, brought in his cow as a mark of fidelity. There was at one

Photographed from the original formerly in State Street Trust Company's collection. Presented to the Nantucket Historical Association

ABRAM QUARY (ABRAM QUADY)
The last Nantucket man with Indian blood in his veins, died November 25, 1854, aged 82 years, and 10 months.

time a well-known Indian preacher in Nantucket who did not always practice what he preached. He used to tell his congregation to act as he said and not as he did. There is an "off island" incident perhaps worthy of introduction here. It was customary for the Indian mothers to strap their children to a board in order to make them straight. Two women had been drinking, and during their orgy they hung their babies to a limb of a tree. Later someone noticed that one of the Indians had unfortunately hung her papoose upside down and of course the child died before help came.

Although the whites on the island treated their neighbors well and there was little warfare among the Indians, nevertheless the latter became greatly reduced chiefly due to a pestilence that was supposed to have been brought there between August, 1763 and February, 1764

Photograph given State Street Trust Company by the late William F. Macy

DORCAS HONORABLE

The last full-blooded Indian on Nantucket, died in the town asylum January 12, 1855. She was born April 27, 1776.

by a wrecked sailor. Their numbers fell from 358 to 136 owing to this disease, which, as was usually the case, did not attack the whites. They continued, however, to whale. Bluefish come and go mysteriously in the waters around Nantucket, and curiously enough, in the same year of the pestilence, this fish, usually so abundant and so frequently seen on the dinner table, entirely disappeared. There is a legend that a dying Indian seer once prophesied that "When the houses of the red men are laid low the bluefish will return." In this prophecy the poor natives are said to have recognized the omen of their own extinction, and many years later, in 1854 on the very day that Abram Quary, the last man on the island to have Indian blood in his veins, died, it is said that two bluefish were caught at Maddequet — the first ones, with few exceptions, since the prediction was made. For some time afterwards they were plentiful. There is a different version of this prophecy, which declares when the last Indian disappeared he would carry the bluefish with him to stock waters of the Happy Hunting Grounds. When Quary, the last half-breed, died, it is said that he took them all with him. Of this Abram Quary, known also as Abram Api Quady, who is connected with this prophecy, there is little known, except that he was respected by all who knew him. He was the son of the notorious Quibby, who was one of the few Indians on the island to be executed for murder, his mother being a half-breed fortune-teller, whose last name Quary quite naturally chose to assume. He lived the life of a hermit in a small hut at Shimmo, on the south shore of the harbor, on a point still known as Abram's and so entered on the maps. He was permitted to cultivate any lands he wished.

Harry B. Turner of the *Inquirer* and *Mirror*, writes to the State Street Trust Company that "He lived the life of a recluse — sad and downhearted at being the last of his race. He seldom came to town, only when in need of provisions, and when his final illness overtook him, he was brought to town and taken care of at 'Our Island Home,' where he passed away." His death came on November 25, 1854, during his eighty-third year.

The distinction of the half-breed Quary of being the last of his tribe on the island is shared, in the eyes of some, by the pure-blooded Darkis Onerable, known also as Dorcas Honorable, who was a servant in the family of John Cartwright, and who died in 1855. Pictures of both these Indians, taken from two excellent likenesses in the Nantucket Athenæum, are shown in illustrations. The Quary print was presented to the Nantucket Historical Society by the State Street Trust Company. The grandfather of Dorcas, Benjamin Tashama, a grandson of the famous Sachem Autopscot already mentioned, was the last Sachem of Nantucket. The latter lived near Gibbs' swamp, and a large stone which stood at the entrance of his house is now at the entrance of the Historical Society's building.

And so the last of a virile race which at one time is said to have been composed of between five hundred and one thousand persons had disappeared from the island — "The greater intellectuality and experience of the one eventually overcame the other," writes Douglas-Lithgow. Obed Macy is probably too severe when he says that "Their only misfortune was their connection with Christians, and their only crime the imitation of their manner."

THE INDIAN AT THE VINEYARD

According to Indian tradition Moshup, the giant divinity, was supposed to have resided long ago on Martha's Vineyard, known by the aborigines as Nöe-pe, signifying "amid the waters." He is said to have warned his people of the coming of the whites. He was fond of making them presents of whales, which from the great doorway of his Devil's Den in the Gay Head cliffs he used to catch at will with his far outstretched arms. After boiling them in his witches' caldron, he would present pieces to his friends. He used to keep the fire alive with the trees within his reach, and perhaps this is one reason why there is nothing higher than a shrub at the Gay Head end of the island. Another legend is that his subjects used to make him presents of tobacco. After a long smoke one day he knocked out the ashes, and the wind being east, they were carried in a heap, thereby forming the island of Nantucket, known by the Vineyarders as the Devil's Ash Heap. It is said that the first Indians to discover Moshup were floated over with a dog on a cake of ice coming from the north. Many tourists search the cliffs for souvenirs of Moshup, and their only reward seems to be the occasional discovery of prehistoric shark remains and fossils. It is doubtful if Nantucketers care to recognize this origin of their island. Moshup's sons were supposed to have been turned into killer whales, his wife, called Old Squant, hiding under a sand-dune at Southwest Head, where, on Indian summer days, smoke appears. This spot is known as the campfire of Old Squant.

A few stories might be introduced here, perhaps, for variety's sake. A descendant of one of the Vineyard Indians was capsized on the way home from New Bedford. Those with him were drowned, but he had a wooden leg and always claimed that he floated on account of it. Banks, in his history of the island, mentions the epitaph of John Doggett, an early native tavern-keeper.

TRAVELLER!

If ever dram to thee was dear,
Drop on John Doggetts grave a Tear,
Who when alive so well did Tend
The Rich, the Poor, the Foe, the Friend;
To every knock, and every call
He said "I'm coming," unto all.
At length Death knocks! poor Doggett cry'd
And said, "I'm coming, Sir!" and Dyed.

Joseph Allen, who escorted the author round the island, in his interesting history of the Vineyard tells a few stories. Showing an example of thrift which might be well for us in America to follow, one of the townships, Chilmark, disagreed as to the location of its schoolhouse and would not vote for a second one. In order to please everyone, it was finally voted to put it on wheels and move it round into different localities so as to give every scholar the same opportunity. Another story of his centers around the installation of a telephone to the mainland. The poles being placed low, some wives hung their washing on the wire, whereupon they were told that "their clothes would be in New Bedford before morning," the wind being strong. A church committee at one time visited a woman who had just given birth to a son, her husband having been at sea for two years. This committee was surprised to receive this reply, "Why, yes, John has written to me several times since he has been away!"

Allen's prize story, though, is of "Uncle Billy Manter's Hoss-less Kerrige." He carted meal to Holmes's Hole and as his load was heavy he rigged a sail in order to assist his old horse. One day he "got kitched sudden in a squall" and "sittin' forward of the canvas, where he couldn't see a thing, Till the wind and rain together, swooped and caught him, wing-and-wing!" Two verses read:

"Down in Holmes's Hole the people ran outdoors to see the sight;
Under sail, a lumber-wagon, comin' like a streak of light!
On the load stood Uncle Billy, keepin' her on even keel,
While beside him restin' caamly, was his hoss, upon the meal!"

By luck the wind backed in time to bring up the wagon at the door of the grain-store. The last verse is:

"Uncle Billy has been sleepin' in his grave for many years,
And his hoss and wagon also have forsook this vale of tears.
But his fame has long outlived him, and the memory is green
Of the fust real hoss-less kerrige that the Vineyard ever seen!"

Our first call was at Christiantown, known also as "God's Acre," which is situated off the northern road to Gay Head and which is reached by a narrow and rough country road. Here is found rather quickly an Indian praying village formed as long ago as 1660. The reservation is now deserted owing to an epidemic of smallpox, having,

Photograph taken by The Mosher Photo Service, Vineyard Haven, Mass., through the kindness of Joseph C. Allen

MAYHEW CHAPEL AND SCHOOL AT CHRISTIANTOWN, MARTHA'S VINEYARD

This reservation, now deserted, served as a home for Christian Indians for two hundred and twenty-eight years. This Indian Chapel school stands in a picturesque setting, with several graveyards nearby. This building was erected in 1829 to replace a similar one that was burned. Beyond on a plateau was their dancing field.

however, served a useful purpose for 228 years. In a picturesque setting stands an old Indian Chapel, erected in 1829 as a place of worship and school with crude seats and pulpit; it replaced an older building. Near by is Pulpit Stone, known as the Mayhew horse block, in memory of Governor Mayhew and his missionaries. A tablet recites that "Within the Boundaries of Manitouwattootan the Ancient Township of the 'Praying Indians' — 'called Christiantown' — 'to commemorate the services of Gov. Thomas Mayhew' . . . And the Boulder Heads the Path to their Burying Ground." There are also headstones to be seen just back of the chapel itself.

By following farther into the woods and by a still rougher road we arrived at a place known as Indian Hill and on a flat field at the top, where there is a summer cottage, the Indians had their dancing field for ceremonial dances. From here one gets a fine view of Naushon, Tarpaulin Cove and Vineyard Sound. The more recent of the inhabitants of Christiantown tried to persuade the older Indians from dancing, but they still continued to pursue their old established custom.

After leaving this delightful spot, my guide, Mr. Allen, drove along the road to Gay Head. This runs past Tea Lane, a pretty road, so named from the fact that a resident used to smuggle in tea for his invalid wife. On the right farther on lived the miller who owned the horseless carriage.

As one gets nearer Gay Head the trees are smaller and smaller, until finally one sees nothing but bushes, as that part of the island is so wind-swept. Approaching the "Head" one passes Powwow Hill and Witch Pond, dark and deep, both situated on the property of Ralph Hornblower. Here is also an Indian altar difficult to locate, and opposite his place across a creek is Toad Rock, the eye serving as a letter-box for the Indians.

At Gay Head is a larger and most interesting Indian Colony owned by the Indians themselves. This settlement was formed in 1642 and has remained an Indian reservation and town ever since. The white man is not seen here. The church and schoolhouse, shown in an illustration, of course, is of special interest to the visitor. Between this crude but well-kept building and the water is South Cemetery, and here the original village of Gay Head used to be situated, but it was found more desirable to move it to higher ground, where the houses are today. Across the road on the Town Hall are two tablets which tell of the sturdiness of the Gay Head Indian. One is in honor of the men who lived there, of whom only one was white, the son of the lighthouse keeper. The other tablet was dedicated by Governor Samuel McCall, "To the Town of Gay Head in recognition of the splendid service to the nation in the war for freedom by furnishing to the army and navy of the United States the largest number of men, in

Through the kindness of Joseph C. Allen
The Mosher Photo Service
Vineyard Haven, Mass.

INDIAN CHAPEL AT GAY HEAD, MARTHA'S VINEYARD
Which is used constantly by the many Indians who reside at the "Head." A tablet on their Town Hall near by records that this community furnished the largest number of men for the World War, in proportion to its population, of any town in New England.

proportion to its population, of any town in New England." It was presented through the *Boston Post*. There are ninety voters in Gay Head today, the largest Indian population of any place in New England with the exception of Old Town in Maine.

A picture here shows the gravestone of Silas Paul, one of the most respected of the Indian ministers at Gay Head; it was taken when the briar bushes were not so high. A few years ago his grave was visited by many persons, owing to the fact that it is the only stone on the island mostly with Indian lettering; but today, unless the undergrowth is kept low, it is not discernible and is as difficult to find as a lost golf ball. The lettering is:

From "Thomas May-   *Courtesy of*
hew, Patriarch to the   *D. Appleton-Century*
Indians," by Lloyd   *Company*
C. M. Hare.

THIS GRAVESTONE OF SILAS PAUL IS NEAR THE GAY HEAD LIGHT HOUSE, BUT IS DIFFICULT TO LOCATE OWING TO THICK BRIAR BUSHES. IT IS THE ONLY HEADSTONE ON THE ISLAND WITH INDIAN LETTERING

YEUUH WOHHOK SIPSIN SIL PAUL
NOHTOBEYONT OK, AGED 49 YEARS
NUP POOP TAH AUGUST 24TH, 1787.

The grave is on the right of the road and near Gay Head lighthouse.

On the way back, on the South

Road, three or four miles from Gay Head, we passed by the district where the Nashuakummuck tribe used to live and where there are many graves. Measles killed them off. It is near the house of Stanley King, President of Amherst. Farther on toward the town, at West Tisbury, we passed the mill of Benjamin Church, where there is a mill dam built by him after King Philip's war. The house is now owned by one of the Mayhew family, so influential in the island's history. Still farther on is an old house built by the son of Myles Standish, who came to Martha's Vineyard and lived there for a time.

"Tawnah! Tawnah!" was the cry that went up when the Vineyard Indians spied a whale. When the first settlers arrived on the island they were surprised to find that these aborigines attacked the whale in their frail birch-bark canoes, which have been said to be models of the first whaleboats of the white men. The redskins spent a great deal of their time on the water and therefore became very expert boatmen. Their method was to use light spears and in this way to tire their prey. The newcomers, however, built larger boats and harpoons, but they had the good judgment to get the Indians to assist them. In this way the Gay Head Indians became connected with this once prosperous industry and held important positions, as high up in rank as boat steerers (harpooners) and officers. Allen, already mentioned, states that one Indian rose to be Captain, but only owing to the death of his superior officer.

A great feat stands to the credit of the Gay Head Indians, in once saving twenty lives. In 1884 the *City of Columbus* went ashore off the "Head" and as Emma Mayhew Whiting writes, "It was the great drama in the lives of the Indians and all things, both before and after, were reckoned in reference to that tragedy." Charles Banks adds a detailed description: "... a life-boat was successfully launched by a crew of Gay Head Indians, consisting of Joseph Peters captain, Samuel Haskins, Samuel Anthony, James Cooper, Moses Cooper, and John Vanderhoop. After battling an hour they were able to bring seven men ashore rescued from the rigging. A second crew manned it, all Indians, except the captain, James T. Mosher. They were Leonard L. Vanderhoop, Thomas C. Jeffers, Patrick Divine, Charles Grimes, and Peter Johnson. They had rescued thirteen men, when the U. S. Revenue Cutter *Dexter* arrived to render assistance." In many an Indian home hangs a medal given on this occasion by the Massachusetts Humane Society.

An Indian who took part in this rescue work, at the suggestion of a resident of the island, has written me an account of his whaling career, including the *Columbus* wreck:

Through the kindness of Joseph C. Allen.

MAYHEW MEMORIAL AT EDGARTOWN, MARTHA'S VINEYARD, NEAR THE WEST TISBURY ROAD

Erected by the D.A.R. of the Island to commemorate the place where Rev. Thomas Mayhew, Jr., bade farewell to his many Indian converts previous to his departure for England in 1657. The vessel was never reported. Previous to the placing of this memorial, it was a custom for any Indian who passed by to drop a stone until a large cairn was created. Some of these stones form a background for the monument.

"I have a Capt. Amos P. Haskins of Gay Head ditty box. He was born in the year of 1816 and got lost to sea in the year of 1847 with all hands. First captain who ever went out of Gayhead.

"I myself was with a man by name Samuel Peters. This Peters was in the ship *Niger* for 18 years. In 1886 I shipped with him as cabin boy and in 1887 Peters died aboard the *Niger* 28 days out of New Bedford. Now this Samuel Peters was one of the men that saved some of the passengers from the Steamer *City of Columbus* that went down off Gay Head. There were five brothers of the Peters' and all whalemen. Out of the five four were buried at sea.

"Then I was with a man by name Judson James. He was with me in the *Niger* in 1886 as well. He is still living but he is in the asylum at Taunton.

"Then I was with a Wallace James of Gay Head. He was a Boat-steerer in 1886 but he became mate of the ship *Niger* in 1890.

"Then there was a man by name Grafton Devine. He was also from Gay Head. He was a boat steerer as well. Then there were a number I know of that came from Gay Head that were whalemen."

Another memorial connected with the Indian is at Edgartown on the old West Tisbury road. Rev. Thomas Mayhew, Jr., the son of the earliest of the "Missionary Mayhews," as they were called, set sail for England in 1657 to raise money. The vessel was never heard from again, but his name and that of the family will live forever on Martha's Vineyard. This Mayhew is described as a "very precious man," "well skilled" and very proficient in the Indian tongue. It is supposed that Hiacoomes of Edgartown, the first convert, placed a stone here at the place where Mayhew said "good-by" to his Indian friends, and afterwards every Indian passing by there laid a stone to his memory until a large cairn was formed. "This rude monument, more eloquent than the greatest cathedral," as expressed by Elizabeth Hare, gradually fell to pieces over a period of years, but in 1901, the D. A. R. dedicated a bronze tablet, set in a large boulder, which was placed besides the stones that remained. The rock was brought from Gay Head by descendants of his beloved natives. Part of the inscription reads:

> THIS ROCK MARKS THE "PLACE ON THE WAYSIDE"
> WHERE THE
> REV. THOMAS MAYHEW, JR.,
> SON OF GOV. MAYHEW,
> FIRST PASTOR OF THE CHURCH OF CHRIST ON MARTHA'S VINEYARD,
> AND THE FIRST MISSIONARY TO THE INDIANS OF NEW
> ENGLAND,
> SOLEMNLY AND AFFECTIONATELY TOOK LEAVE OF THE INDIANS,
> WHO, IN LARGE NUMBERS, HAD FOLLOWED HIM DOWN
> FROM THE WESTERN PART OF THE ISLAND,
> BEING HIS LAST WORSHIP AND INTERVIEW WITH THEM
> BEFORE EMBARKING FOR ENGLAND IN 1657,
> FROM WHENCE HE NEVER RETURNED
> NO TIDINGS EVER COMING FROM THE SHIP OR ITS PASSENGERS.
> IN LOVING REMEMBRANCE OF HIM
> THOSE INDIANS RAISED THIS PILE OF STONE, 1657–1901.

It may be of interest to know that there is a tower in Lowndes County, Mississippi, called Mayhew Station, "in memory of the excellent and devoted men who so successfully preached the Gospel to the Indians on Martha's Vineyard."

From a Currier & Ives print
INDIAN DANCE BEFORE A BALL GAME

INDIAN GAMES

"Skilled was he in sports and pastimes,
In the merry dance of snowshoes,
In the play of quoits and ball-play;
Skilled was he in games of hazard,
In all games of skill and hazard,
Pugasaing, the Bowl and Counters,
Kuntassoo, the Game of Plum-stones."

(These words by Longfellow in "The Song of Hiawatha," describing the warrior Yenadizze, seem fitting to introduce this account of Indian games.)

It does not require much imagination to visualize a game of football, hockey or lacrosse (whatever it was then called) being played on one of our sandy beaches such as Nantasket, Ipswich, Revere, Manchester, Scituate, Narragansett, Rye or other places New England offered. A long smooth stretch was necessarily required; for we are told that the goal posts were often placed as far apart as a mile, that sometimes whole villages and even tribes competed, and that the game would often continue for several days. No one knows how long this sport was played by the aborigines in this country, or where it originated.

The accounts we studied show that lacrosse, with its variations that might mean football or hockey, was played throughout this country. Platter, or dice, which we will mention later, was also indulged in very generally, and the curious game of Straw or Indian cards was found apparently only in the south and west. The early English explorers found the same sports in New England and Virginia that the French found in Canada, with the addition of football, which was especially adaptable to our New England beaches.

We shall attempt to quote as many references as there are concerning the New England games, and outside of this district we will mention the accounts that seem to us of special interest. The Indian name applied to football was almost as long as the playgrounds themselves. Roger Williams, who gives us the best descriptions of the various aboriginal sports of New England, refers to "Pasuckquakohowaûog," as meaning "they meet to foot-ball." He describes it as played by the Narragansetts of Rhode Island, among whom he lived for many years: "Besides, they have great meetings of foot-ball playing, only in Summer, towne against towne, upon some broad sandy shoare, free from stones, or upon some soft heathie plot, because of their naked feet, at which they have great stakings, but seldome quarrell." In some localities the game was played during the winter on the ice, but it is not explained how the players were able to keep their feet. William Wood in his "New England's Prospect" has handed down an interesting and longer account of the same pastime: "Their Goales be a mile long placed on the sands, which are as even as a board; their ball is no bigger than a hand-ball, which sometimes they mount in the Aire with their naked feete, sometimes it is swayed by the multitude; sometimes also it is two dayes before they get a Goale, then they marke the ground they winne, and beginne there the next day. Before they come to this sport, they paint themselves, even as when they goe to warre, in pollicie to prevent future mischiefe, because no man should know him that moved his patience or accidentally hurt his person, taking away the occasion of studying revenge. Before they begin their armes be disordered, and hung upon some neighbouring tree, after which they make a long scrowle on the sand, over which they shake loving hands, and with laughing hearts scuffle for victorie. While the men play the boyes pipe, and the women dance and sing trophies of their husbands conquests; all being done a feast summons their departure. It is most delight to see them play, in smaller companies, when men may view their swift footemanship, their curious tossings of this Ball, their flouncing into the water, their lubberlike wrestling, having no cunning at all in that kind, one English being able to beate ten Indians at footeball."

From "The Indian Races of North and South America," by Charles De Wolf Brownell

AN INDIAN BALL GAME, OR LACROSSE

There seems to be a great deal of difference among writers as to the distances between goals in this game. We have seen that Wood places them a mile apart. These "Goales," to quote Wood again, are "all be-hung with Wampompeage, Mowhackies, Beaver skins, and blacke Otter skinnes. It would exceede the beleefe of many to relate the worth of one Goale." The number of the players engaged also seems to have varied greatly, and appears to have been governed by the circumstances that existed. The largest figure we have seen mentioned was two thousand. Others speak of forty or eighty or so on a side, while others mention three or four hundred a side. The ball itself, apparently, was originally made of wood, and later of deer-skin stuffed with deer's hair. When the sides were evenly matched the game lasted all afternoon and sometimes, as we have heard, it lasted for several days. Our modern game of football, rough as it is, must be mere child's play compared to this sport of the Indian.

All writers agree that this form of exercise tended to make the participants alert and trained them for the warpath and also to avoid the tomahawks of their antagonists. Davis concludes "that it was rather a contest of grave importance to the players than a mere pastime."

On one occasion, at least, the game of football was used as a ruse to capture a fort at a place called Michilimackinac, in Canada. Parkman describes the event very vividly: "Rushing and striking, tripping their adversaries, or hurling them to the ground, they pursued the animating contest amid the laughter and applause of the spectators. Suddenly, from the midst of the multitude, the ball soared into the air and, descending in a wide curve, fell near the pickets of the fort. This was no chance stroke. It was part of a preconcerted scheme to insure the surprise and destruction of the garrison. As if in pursuit of the ball, the players turned and came rushing, a maddened and tumultuous throng, toward the gate. In a moment they had reached it. The amazed English had no time to think or act. The shrill cries of the ball-players were changed to the ferocious war-whoop. The warriors snatched from the squaws the hatchets which the latter, with this design, had concealed beneath their blankets. Some of the Indians assailed the spectators without, while others rushed into the fort, and all was carnage and confusion."

The Indians certainly had the gambling spirit. Roger Williams tells us that they sometimes staked their money, clothes, homes, food and even themselves if they were single. Winslow in his "Good Newes from England," writes that "they use gaming as much as anywhere and will play away all, even their skin from their backs, yea their wives' skin also, though it may be they are many miles distant from them, as I myself have seen." Gookin at a later date says: "They are addicted to gaming and will, in that vein, play away all they have." Longfellow in "Hiawatha" refers to their eagerness to gamble:

> "Played for dresses, weapons, wampum,
> Played till midnight, played till morning.
> Played until the Yenadizze,
> Till the cunning Pau-Puk-Keewis,
> Of their treasures had despoiled them,
> Of the best of all their dresses,
> Shirts of deer-skin, robes of ermine,
> Belts of wampum, crests of feathers,
> Warlike weapons, pipes and pouches."

"Often," writes Andrew McFarland Davis, who has studied this subject, "he will put up not only his own possessions, but the property of his friends and neighbors." He adds: "There are writers who seek to reduce the impressions of the extravagance indulged in by the Indians at these games. The concurrence of testimony is to the effect that there was no limit to which they would not go. Their last blanket or bead,

From a Currier & Ives print

INDIAN BALL PLAYERS

the clothing on their backs, their wives and children, their own liberty were sometimes hazarded; and if the chances of the game went against them the penalty was paid with unflinching firmness." Possibly this statement may refer to the Canadian Indians, for Lescarbot who came to Canada explains that the delivery of the wagered wives was not always easily accomplished, but that attempt would at least be faithfully made and was often successful. Perhaps this may have been an Indian method of divorce! Another author states that he has seen a loser return home after the game "as naked as your hand." Even more than this, the reputation of a whole tribe or village depended upon the result. Perrot, in speaking of the games as played in the West, states that they are so keen for football that they "will neglect food and drink, not only to join in a game, but even to look at one."

Platter or dice was the second most popular game among the Indians of this country, and of this sport as played in New England and the place in which it was played, Roger Williams, who divides the game into two classes, public and private, says: "They have a kind of Dice which are Plumb stones painted, which they cast in a Tray with a mighty noyse and sweating. Their publique games, are solemnized with the meeting of hundreds; sometimes thousands, and consist of many varieties, none of which I durst ever be present at that I might not countenance and partake of their folly after I once saw the evill of them. The chiefe Gamesters amongst them much desire to make their Gods side with them . . . therefore I have seen them keepe as a precious stone a piece of Thunderbolt, which is like unto a Chrystall, which they dig out of the ground under some Tree, Thunder Smitten, and from this stone they have an opinion of successe, and I have not heard any of these prove loosers, which I conceive may be Satans policie, and God's holy Justice to harden them for their not rising higher from the Thunder-bolt, to the God that sends or shoots it."

He then describes their gambling place: "This Arbour or Play house is made of long poles set in the Earth, four square, sixteen or twentie foot high, on which they hang great store of their stringed money, have great staking towne against towne, and two chosen out

Photographed from "Letters and Notes on the Manners, Customs and Condition of the North American Indians," by George Catlin

BALL PLAYING — BALL UP

of the rest by course to play the Game at this kind of Dice, in the midst of all their abettors, with great shouting and solemnity: . . ."

Roger Williams ends his chapter on gaming with several amusing lines:

> "Our English Gamesters scorne to stake
> Their clothes as Indians do,
> Nor yet themselves, alas, yet both
> Stake soules and lose them too.
>
> O fearfull Games! the Divell stakes
> But Strawes, and Toyes and Trash,
> For what is All, compar'd with Christ,
> But Dogs meat and Swines wash?
>
> Man stakes his Jewell-darling soule,
> (His owne most wretched foe)
> Ventures, and loseth all in sport
> At one most dreadfull throw."

Wood in his "New England Prospect" speaks of the Indians in this locality as "spending halfe their dayes in gaming and lazing" and of course the Dice game with its variations was very conducive to this manner of living. The same author mentions two other games, Puim, played with short sticks called Puims, and "hee that is a noted gamster, hath a great hole in his eare wherein hee carries his Puims in defiance of his antagonists." The other indoor sport referred to is Hubbub which resembles Dice. "Hubbub," writes Wood, "is five small Bones in a small smooth Tray, . . . which they place on the Ground, against which violently thumping the Platter, the Bones mount, changing colours with the windy whisking of their Hands too and fro; which action in that sport they much use, smiting themselves on the

Photographed from "Letters and Notes on the Manners, Customs, and Condition of the North American Indians," by George Catlin

BALL PLAYING — BALL ON GROUND

Breast, and Thighs, crying out, Hub, Hub, Hub; they may be heard play at this Game a quarter of a Mile off: . . . They are so bewitch'd with these two Games (football and dice) that they will lose sometimes all they have; Beaver, Moose-skinnes, Kettles, Wampompeage, Mowhackies, Hatchets, Knives, all is confiscate by these two Games."

Sometimes a fast was proclaimed for several days before the game was started, and it was customary for all to meet together in some cabin and to hold a powwow in order to find out what was to be the result of the contest.

Longfellow describes the game of "Bowl and Counters" as it was called by some of the Indian tribes, as follows:

"All the game of Bowl and Counters,
Pugasaing, with thirteen pieces.
White on one side were they painted,
And vermilion on the other;
Two Kenabeeks or great serpents,
Two Ininewug or wedge-men,
One great war-club, Pugamaugun,
And one slender fish, the Keego,
Four round pieces, Ozawabeeks,
And three Sheshebwug or ducklings.
All were made of bone and painted,
All except the Ozawabeeks;
These were brass, on one side burnished,
And were black upon the other.
In a wooden bowl he placed them,
Shook and jostled them together,
Threw them on the ground before him."

The game of dice often began with singing. As in lacrosse or hockey "it was prescribed," according to Mr. Davis, "as a remedy for sickness or in consequence of dreams, and the sufferer in whose behalf the game was played was borne to the cabin in which it was to take place. Preliminary fasting and continence were observed, and every effort made that superstitition could suggest to discover who would be the lucky thrower and who could aid the caster by his presence at the contest. Old men, unable to walk thither, were brought up on the shoulders of the young men that their presence might be propitious to the chances of the game." Continuing, he says that both the players and spectators lose in some degree their very senses at it. "The players address the dice and beat themselves on their breasts. The spectators during the same period filled the air with shouts and invoked aid from their own protecting powers, while in the same breath they poured forth imprecations on those of their adversaries." Usually there were two players on each side representing a tribe or village, and their selection is described by Mr. Davis: "The prevailing motives in their choice were generally based upon some superstitious belief in their luck. Perhaps this one had dreamed that he would win. Perhaps that one was believed to possess some magic power, or some secret ointment which when applied to the dice would cause them to turn up favorably for his side."

The excitement reached a high pitch especially when all depended upon a particular throw. Its duration was often as long as five or six days, according to Charlevoix. As in other sports the Indians were philosophical concerning their losses. Brebeuf describes a party of redskins that wagered and lost all its leggings and that returned to their village in three feet of snow apparently almost as cheerful as if they had been the victors. The women often carried on the game by themselves, but never as strenuously.

The third most important of the Indian games was known as Straw, Reeds or Rushes, and was the Indian's game of cards, according to Roger Williams. Sometimes it was known also as Arithmetic. New England writers do not refer to it, but it was undoubtedly played in most sections of the country. It was a game of very quick calculation, and as one person put it, "he who best knows how to add and subtract, to multiply and divide with these straws will surely win. To do this, use and practice are necessary, for these savages are nothing less than good calculators." The game consisted in separating the straws, usually short sticks and considered to be very valuable, into piles that contained an uneven number. One writer describes this competition as follows: "The art is, to discover, upon sight, how many you have, and what you throw to him that plays with you. Some are so expert at their numbers, that they will tell ten times together, what they throw out of their hands. Although the whole play is carried on with the quickest motion it is possible to use, yet some are so expert at this Game, as to win great Indian Estates by this Play." Davis writes of it: "The player who was to make the division into two heaps, with many contortions of the body and throwing about of the arms, and with constant utterances to propitiate his good luck, would make a division of the straws with a pointed bone or some similar instrument, himself taking one of the divisions

Photographed from "The Histoire of Travaile into Virginia Britannia," by William Strachey, Gent.
AN INDIAN DANCE

while his adversary took the other. They would then rapidly separate the straws into parcels numbering ten each and determine from the fractional remainders, who had the odd number." The counting was done by tens much like the lightning figurers, who in adding a long column of numbers, group together those that total exactly ten. Ferland considered that "Memory, calculation and quickness of eyesight were necessary for success." All who ever witnessed these exhibitions have been surprised at the quickness of the Indian in counting the straws that were thrown, in order to detect whether the pile cast contained an odd or even number. One does not think of the Indian of the early days as a quick calculator. The game was carried on in the largest cabins of the chiefs. The betting was done exactly as in faro, and as in all of the aboriginal indoor games it was the usual custom to continue the play until one side had lost all its possessions. We are told that substitutes could be put in at any time.

There were various other games played among the tribes, and undoubtedly by the New England Indians. Roger Williams describes a "kinde of solemne, publike meeting, wherein they lie under the trees, in a kinde of Religious observation, and have a mixture of Devotions and sports. . . . Their chiefest Idoll of all for sport and game, is . . . towards Harvest, when they set up a long house . . . sometimes an hundred, sometimes two hundred foot long upon a plaine neer the Court . . . where many thousands, men and women meet, where he that goes in danceth in the sight of all the rest; and is prepared with money, coats, small breeches, knives, or what hee is able to reach to, and gives these things away to the Poore."

In some places Chunkee or Hoop and Pole was played, and also a game of ball much resembling our Basket Ball, which was tossed into the air and over the goals by the hands. They also had their Javelin throwing, and any Indian who failed to hit the mark forfeited the hurled weapon. Many other guessing games, of course, were played, too numerous to mention. Jackstones, Blind-man's-buff, running and swimming races, wrestling, jumping rope and tug-of-war were resorted to as pastimes. When the first settlers came to Canada they were amused to see little Indian children sliding down hills on flat

Kindness Charles D. Childs

INDIAN GAME OF THE ARROW OR ARCHERY

pieces of wood strapped together and turned up in front. The present toboggan is modeled after the old Indian type.

Spinning top was a favorite amusement of the children, and when the cold weather came they could carry on their amusement on the ice. We read of the natives who would try to run around their homes before the top stopped spinning. Sometimes the top was kept in motion by means of continual whipping with a small buckskin whip. The Indian offspring have been reported as skilled at trundling hoop, and one writer from the West makes the statement that many of the younger children could "stop the progress of the hoop when going with great velocity, by driving the pointed arrow into its edge." This act of markmanship, though, must have been rather unusual.

Among some tribes the women held foot-races and one account, coming from the South, might well be quoted: "At the appointed time everybody in camp assembled to witness the contest. Among the competitors was the Apache girl, Ish-kay-nay, a clean-limbed, handsome girl of 17, who had always refused marriage, and she was the favorite among the whites. Each runner was tightly girded with a broad belt, and looked like a race horse. Ten entered for the halfmile stake, which was a gaudy piece of calico for a dress or shirt, as the case might be. At the word they went off like rockets, Nah-kah-yen leading handsomely, and Ish-kay-nay bringing up the rear, but running as clean and easy as a greyhound. Within 400 yards of the goal she closed the gap, went by like a steam engine, and got in an easy winner, 6 yards ahead of all competitors."

JOURNEY CAKE — JONNY-CAKE

The original spelling of the word "Jonny-Cake," described by Thomas R. Hazard in his amusing "Jonny-Cake Papers of 'Shepherd Tom'" as "the favorite food of the gods," was "Journey-Cake," that is, cake made in haste for a journey. This earlier name was given to this well-known food for the reason that it could be prepared quickly and could be carried very easily by the Indians when they were making a long journey. Hazard explains how the name happened to be changed: "This name journey-cake," he says, "was retained until the close of the War of Independence, about which time, in compliance with the prayers of memorials from the women of Connecticut and Rhode Island to the respective Legislatures of these commonwealths — the term journey, as applied to the favorite food of the gods and of the Yankee nation, was abrogated by sovereign authority, and that of 'jonny' substituted in its place in honor of Governor Jonathan Trumbull, the honored and trusted friend of General Washington, who always addressed the sterling patriot with the affectionate pet name of 'Brother Jonathan.'" The author of these Papers adds this further remark: "The Southern epicures crack a good deal about hoe-cakes and hominy made from their white flint corn, the Pennsylvanians of their mush, the Boston folks of their Boston brown bread, whilst one Joel Barlow, of New Haven, or somewhere else in Connecticut, used to sing a long song in glorification of New England hasty pudding; but none of these reputed luxuries are worthy of holding a candle to an old-fashioned Narragansett jonny-cake made by an old-time Narragansett colored cook. . . ." Phillis, negro family cook mentioned by Hazard, according to this authority made the best jonny-cake of anyone alive. It had to be made, of course, on a red oak jonny-cake board. He describes it as the "best article of farinaceous food that was ever partaken of by mortal man."

"Journey" cake was made in large quantity by the Indians of the Narragansett Country, now comprised in the State of Rhode Island. Not only has the Indian name, in a slightly changed form, come down to us, but this far-famed cake, which is supposed by Rhode Islanders to be made to perfection only in the Southern Counties of that State, is even today one of our most delicious dishes. This article of food was used by the Indians of the interior on their long marches to and from their summer resorts on the Southern shores of the Atlantic, the chief of which were at Narragansett and Newport. One of their stopping places between there and Cape Cod was at New Bedford, and the supposed location of these halts, directly behind the Dartmouth Historical Society, has been well named Johnny Cake Hill, for here they used to feed upon the journey cakes which they brought with them.

A well-known resident of that city, George H. Tripp, formerly the head of the Free Public Library, has sent us some further information on this subject which he found in "An American Glossary." It reads: "1863 The real name is Journey cake; that is, cake made in haste for a journey. Johnny cake! We might as well call it Tommy or Pelatiah cake! — *Phila. Public Ledger*, May 21.

"1848 Corn-meal, pounded in a wooden mortar, or ground in a handmill of steel, supplied the place of flour . . . The dough, when

39

properly prepared, was spread upon a piece of shaved clapboard from three to four inches wide, and from fifteen to twenty inches long, and baked upon the hearth. When both sides were perfectly done, it was called journey-cake or Johnny-cake. A journey-cake board was an indispensable implement of frontier cooking. Johnny-cake and pone were the only varieties of bread used among the early frontier settlements for breakfast and dinner . . . When milk was not plenty, the lack was supplied by the substantial dish of hommony, or pounded corn thoroughly boiled."

No-cake, made of pounded parched Indian corn, was a great Indian dish "in which," according to Mr. Hazard, "was concentrated such inexpressible sweetness and life-sustaining power that the aborigines of New England, when hunting or on the war path, could carry forty days' provisions each on their backs without inconvenience." The No-Cake family, the last survivors of the Narragansett Indians, is now extinct in Washington County. Remnants of the tribe were at one time located at the Indian Reservation at Charlestown, in that county.

Roger Williams speaks of parched meal, which resembled Jonny Cake and adds: "It is a readie very wholesome food which they eate with a little water, hot or cold; I have travelled with neare 200 of them at once neare 100 miles through the woods, every man carrying a little basket of this (parched meal — Nokehick) at his back, and sometimes in a hollow leather girdle about his middle, sufficient for a man for three or four daies." He speaks then of tobacco and says that they take it "for two causes; first, against the rheume, which causes the toothake, which they are impatient of: secondly, to revive and refresh them, they drinking nothing but water."

The Indians evidently made up for the scarcity of food while traveling by gorging when they reached their destination, for William Wood in his "New England's Prospect" gives this quite unattractive yet vivid description: "At home they will eate till their bellies stand South, ready to split with fulnesse, it being their fashion, to eate all at sometimes, and sometimes nothing at all in two or three days, wise providence being a stranger to their wilder dayes."

QUEEN AWASHONKS

Queen Awashonks was more tractable, kindly and submissive and rather less warlike, dominating and relentless a character than her compatriot Weetamoe, described in our first Indian booklet. These two Queens were the Indian Amazons of their day and both had at their command bands of braves which made them equally powerful in the Narragansett country. Both belonged to the Wampanoag tribe and ruled over neighboring territories. Awashonks was known as the Squaw Sachem of Sogkonate, now chiefly included in the town of Little Compton and usually known as Sakonnet. This tract of land is situated on the northeast side of Narragansett Bay, on the southeast end of the island of Rhode Island. It is supposed that she usually spent her summers in Falmouth making an occasional excursion to Gay Head on the Vineyard, where it is believed she had friends.

The first official notice of her was on July 24, 1671, when evidently she herself appeared at Plymouth with others of her following and signed an agreement of submission, and a month later forty-two of her chiefs signified in writing their approval of her action. There is in existence a copy of a letter written by her at this time and addressed to Governor Prince of Massachusetts in which she explained that she intended to send in all her six guns, but that two of them were so large the messengers were unable

Photographed by Rev. T. E. Thompson

AWASHONKS MEMORIAL, LITTLE COMPTON, RHODE ISLAND, LOCATED IN WILBUR'S PARK
Her grave is in the Old Indian Burying Ground, half a mile distant, on the property of Dr. Franklin C. Southworth.

to carry them and that "since then an Indian, known by the name of Broad-faced-will stole one of them out of the wigwam in the night, and is run away with it to Mount Hope . . . Honored sir, I shall not trouble you further, but deserving your peace and prosperity, in which I look at my own to be included, I remain, your unfeigned servant." Of course the letter was written by an interpreter. Governor Prince made a tardy reply to this note assuring her that the English would befriend her.

About a year before King Philip's war broke out Benjamin Church, later to become Colonel and the Colony leader in that war, moved from Duxbury and took up his abode on the Sogkonate peninsula in the midst of Awashonks' people, with whom he became very friendly. Here he hoped to settle down quietly and do some farming, but this was not to be; for in the spring of 1675 rumors of trouble were in the air. Philip dispatched six messengers to the "Queen" to enlist her services and her warriors on his side in the approaching conflict. On June 15th she decided to hold a council of war and a dance and called her men together, and as she knew Captain Church well, she gave him also the opportunity to be present. The latter with an interpreter, Charles Hazelton, joined the gathering where, to use his own words, he found that she "in a foaming Sweat was leading the Dance. But she was no sooner sensible of (his) arrival, but she broke off, sat down, calls her Nobles round her, orders (him) to be invited into her presence. Compliments being past, and each one taking Seats." Awashonks told Church that Philip had sent word that the "Umpames," the Indian name for the people of Plymouth, were collecting a great army to invade his lands. Church had recently come from that place and reassured her on this point, adding that he would never have settled in that territory had he thought there was any idea of invasion. This answer seemed to convince her of his truthfulness, and she thereupon ordered the six visiting warriors into her presence. Church was disconcerted at their formidable appearance, for he wrote that they approached "with their Faces Painted, and their Hair Trim'd up in Comb-fashion, with their Powder-horns, and Shot-bags at their backs; which among that Nation is the posture and figure of preparedness for War." Awashonks repeated to them the information given by Captain Church, which irritated Philip's ambassadors so greatly that they lost their tempers and withdrew. Much talk ensued, but the Squaw Sachem was able to quiet them. She then told Church that Philip had sent word by them that if she would not enter into the Indian confederacy he would send his warriors over into her lands to kill the English cattle and burn their houses, which would provoke the newcomers to attack her as the probable author of these deeds. Church told her he very much regretted this turn in affairs. He now approached the warlike Mount Hopes and thought it well to feel of their bullet-pouches. Finding them full he thereupon inquired of them what they were going to do with their powder and bullets, to which he received the scoffing reply, "to shoot pigeons with." The Captain then made the unfortunate remark to Awashonks that if King Philip had made up his mind upon war, her best course to follow "would be to knock these six Mount Hopes on the head, and shelter herself under the protection of the English." She was naturally very angry at this suggestion and, had she acted hastily in making her decision, her enmity would have been a serious blow to the cause of the colonists. One of the Sogkonates, "Little-eyes" by name, endeavored to draw Church aside and kill him, but his tribesmen prevented his doing so.

After some deliberation Awashonks accepted the recommendation of Captain Church to submit to the colonists and concluded not to take part in a war against the English that would ultimately prove disastrous, but requested him to repair at once to Plymouth and tell the authorities of her decision. He promised to return soon. The Queen was so grateful for his advice that she sent two of her trusted men with him. They reached their destination on June 7, 1675. On his way he met at Pocasset Weetamoe's husband, Peter, who confirmed the prob-

BENJAMIN CHURCH

From "Biography and History of the Indians of North America, from its First Discovery," by Samuel G. Drake

COLONEL BENJAMIN CHURCH
The most daring and bravest leader among the Colonists in the days of Indian warfare. To him more than to any other officer was due the final victory over the enemy at the Great Swamp Fight. He was a resident of Plymouth, and later moved to Rhode Island. His burial place is at Little Compton.

ability of war and later he fell in with Weetamoe herself, as we have mentioned in our first volume.

As luck would have it, the war broke out immediately and all communication with Awashonks was therefore at an end. Church found out later that not hearing from him she had cast her lot rather unwillingly with King Philip, having been won over evidently by his early successes. After recovering from a wound received in the great swamp fight of December, 1675, Church resolved again to go to war and took passage for Barnstable, reaching Plymouth early in June of the following year. He received a hearty welcome and was at once given command of a body of troops about to be sent out. In going from Sogkonesset, now Woods Hole, to Rhode Island, he noticed at Sogkonate Point some Indians and recognized his neighbor George, who was the friendly native to guide him home from Awashonks' camp. George told Church that the Squaw Sachem was near Tiverton only three miles distant and desired to see him and conclude a peace, whereupon a meeting was arranged, probably on June 10th, at a certain place in the lower end of Captain Richmond's farm, known as "Treaty Rock." Church's Point is about half a mile distant. The English officer always believed he still could detach the Seconets could he only have a chance to interview them, and he also felt that Awashonks and her men would never have joined with Philip had he been able to see her again before the war started. The authorities at Rhode Island urged him not to undertake this mission, and even refused to permit one of their interpreters to go with him. So with his own servant and two Indians, the ever useful bottle of rum and a roll of tobacco, he set out from Woods Hole to the appointed conference. The Indians seemed at first friendly, but soon disappeared, apparently for consultation. Suddenly, without any warning, Church writes that "at once a-rose up a great body of Indians, who had lain hid in the grass that was as high as a mans waste and gathered round them, till they had clos'd them in, being all arm'd with Guns, Spears, Hatchets, etc. with their hair trim'd and faces painted, in their Warlike appearance." Although the pictures of Colonel Church look most unwarlike, he was nevertheless the most daring and bravest leader in the Colony at that time and apparently on this occasion, as at other times, he seemed undismayed at this ferocious display. Approaching Awashonks he mentioned the possibility of peace, and asked her if it was customary in such cases to appear in such hostile array. At a word from their leader they put aside their guns and sat down. Church, who wrote his book on the war in the third person, continued the interview in these words:

"He pulled out his Callebash and asked Awashonks, Whether she had lived so long at Wetuset (she had evidently spent that winter at Wachusett) as to forget to drink Occapechees; and drinking to her, he perceived that she watch'd him very diligently, to see (as he thought) whether he swallowed any of the Rhum; he offered her the Shell, but she desired him to drink again first, He then told her, There was no poison in it, and pouring some into the Palm of his hand sup'd it up, and took the Shell and drank to her again, and drank a good Swig which indeed was no more than he needed. Then they all standing up, he said to Awashonks, You wont drink for fear there should be poison in it; And then handed it to a little ill look'd fellow, who catched it readily enough, and as greedily would have swallowed the Liquor when he had it at his mouth; But Mr. Church catch'd him by the throat and took it from him, asking him, Whether he intended to swallow Shell and all? And then handed it to Awashonks, she ventured to take a good hearty dram, and pass'd it among her Attendants. The Shell being emptied, he pulled out his Tobacco, and having distributed it, they began to talk." When a few rounds of drinks had been quaffed Awashonks admitted she would not have joined Philip had Church returned to her camp.

After a display of enmity against the visitor on the part of a belligerent warrior, an agreement was arrived at by which the Indian leader agreed to serve the English "in what way she was able," provided "Plimouth would firmly engage to them, that they and all of them, and their wives and children should have their lives spared, and none of them transported out of the country." Church assured her the people of Plymouth would live up to this provision of the treaty and they did so. The chief Captain of the Sogkonates now arose and acknowledged the great respect he had for Church and then stated: "Sir, if you will please accept of me and my men, and will head us, we'll fight for you, and will help you to Philip's head before the Indian Corn be ripe." This prophecy was to be later fulfilled, but not actually by one of the Sogkonates. Again we learn the value of a solemn promise of an Indian, for this band continued on the side of the whites during the remainder of the conflict, taking part in a number of expeditions. It was said that Philip never again smiled when he heard that Awashonks, who was probably a distant relative, had deserted his party.

Church now sent Peter, a son of the Squaw Sachem and chief captain, to Plymouth with a statement of all that had taken place, and he himself set off on June 27th to meet Major Bradford and the Colonial troop at Pocasset. Bradford asked Church to tell Awashonks to come to Punkateese and on the way Church met a number of straying Indians who gave him various information. One of them is described as being weighted down by a "Quarter of a Cow on his Back and her Tongue in his Pocket." Awashonks was ordered to join them at Punkateese, but complications ensued. Church now decided to look her up. He first went to Sandwich and, not finding Awashonks and her tribesmen, continued on to Wareham, where he discovered them still farther south on the shore of Buzzards Bay enjoying an Indian field day or picnic. Church and his few followers dismounted from their horses and crept through the bushes, not being sure whether they were friend or foe. Peering over the precipice the Colonial officer wrote that they "saw a vast company of Indians, of all Ages and Sexs, some on Horseback running races, some at Foot-ball, some catching Eels & Flat-fish in the water, some Clamming, &c. but which way with safety to find out what Indians they were, they were at a loss." By means of two straggling Indians they found out that a redskin they knew, called Jack Havens, was among their party and, sending for him, Church learned that they were none other than Awashonks and her tribesmen. Church then sent word that he "designed to Sup with her in the Evening, and to lodge in her Camp that

Night." Upon their arrival, to quote again Church, who still uses the third person in his account of his adventures, they were "immediately conducted to a shelter, open on one side, wither Awashonks and her chiefs soon came & paid their Respects: and the Multitudes gave shouts as made the heavens to ring." Now began a celebration which has been so vividly portrayed that we will let the same author continue it in his own words: "It being now about Sun-setting, or near the dusk of the Evening; the Netops (friends) came running from all quarters loaden with the tops of dry Pines & the like combustible matter making a huge pile thereof, near Mr. Churches shelter, on the open side thereof; but by this time Supper was brought in, in three dishes, vix. a curious young Bass, in one dish, Eels & Flat-fish in a second, and Shell-fish in a third, but neither Bread nor Salt to be seen at Table. But by that time Supper was over, the mighty pile of Pine Knots and Tops, &c. was fired, and all the Indians great and small gathered in a ring round it. Awashonks with the oldest of her People Men and Women mix'd, kneeling down made the first ring next the fire, and all the lusty, stout Men standing up made the next: and then all the Rabble in a confused Crew surrounded on the outside. Then the chief Captain step'd in between the rings and the fire, with a Spear in one hand and a Hatchet in the other, danced round the fire, and began to fight with it, making mention of all the several Nations & Companies of Indians in the Country that were Enemies to the English; & at naming of every particular Tribe of Indians, he would draw out & fight a new fire brand, & at his finishing his fight with each particular fire-brand, would bow to him and thank him; and when he had named all the several Nations and Tribes, and fought them all he stuck down his Spear and Hatchet, and came out; and another stept in and acted over the same dance, with more fury, if possible than the first; and when about half a dozen of their chiefs had thus acted their parts, The Captain of the Guard stept up to Mr. Church and told him, They were making Souldiers for him, and what they had been doing was all one Swearing of them (the principle of enlistment) and having in that manner ingaged all the lusty stout men. Awashonks & her chiefs came to Mr. Church; and told him, That now they were all ingaged to fight for the English, and he might call forth all, or any of them at any time as he saw occasion to fight the Enemy; and presented him with a very fine Firelock."

Church accepted the offer, selected a few of her men, and started out for Plymouth early the next morning. He received a commission, and with sixty English volunteers and one hundred and forty of the Sogkonates, he made a number of successful expeditions which through modesty he has never properly narrated. This brave fighter and victor of many battles died at his home in Little Compton on January 17, 1718, from the effects of a fall from his horse.

A New Bedford whale ship was named Awashonks, for this well-known woman who held domain not far from that port.

KING PHILIP AND THE TAUNTON TREATY

A very unusual scene was enacted on April 12, 1671, in the Meeting House on Taunton Green when the English Commissioners from the Bay and Plymouth governments met King Philip and his

From a painting in the New England Mutual Life Insurance Co.
KING PHILIP — THE LAST OF THE WAMPANOAGS
Signing the Treaty of 1671 with the Massachusetts Bay Colony in the Old Church at Taunton.

leading counsellors. The occasion must have rivalled in picturesqueness the first Thanksgiving in Plymouth when the Pilgrims in the year 1621 sat down for dinner with some friendly Indians, as shown in the frontispiece. Several writers have described this dramatic meeting. One account was written by Francis Baylies: "On one side were arranged the austere puritan English with formal garbs, close shorn hair and solemn countenance, looking hostility and defiance, yet with a shade of submissive devotion, which showed that they were willing to put their trust in the God of battles. On the other side appeared the tawny and ferocious countenances of the Indian warriors; their long black hair hanging down their backs; their small and sunken eyes gleaming with serpent fires; their persons covered with belts of wampum, and fantastic ornaments, exhibiting a combination of every gaudy color. The sober and silent demeanor of the English, and the strange and wild deportment of the Indians, presented a contrast the more remarkable, inasmuch as they had lived together for fifty years." The other description from Bryant & Gay's History follows: "One half of the sanctuary was filled by the painted warriors, with feathered crests and beaded trappings — sombre, silent, wary. On the other side was the counterfoil of Englishmen in broad hats, muskets, bandoliers, cuirasses, and long rapiers, — a picture from the age of Cromwell. Never before or since did the plain roof of a New England meeting-house cover a contrast so highly colored in costume and idea. In those pews, Boston compelled Philip to promise to deliver up all the English arms in the possession of his tribe."

The occasion for this conference was the desire of the Massachusetts authorities to find out whether the leader of the Wampanoags was really preparing for hostilities, which they had heard to be the case. They also feared that Plymouth was becoming too excited and might in some way bring on a war. The colonists believed they might be able to prevent the threatening King Philip war.

Accordingly three representatives from Boston, William Davis, William Hudson and Thomas Brattle, met Governor Thomas Prince of Plymouth, who had with him Josiah Winslow and Constant Southworth, after having summoned King Philip to meet them at Taunton. The Indian Chieftain, with his band of warriors armed and painted as if ready for war, approached within four miles of the town, where he established his camp. He thereupon dispatched messengers to the English, inviting them to meet him. The Governor quite naturally preferred Philip to come into town, and it was finally arranged for him to do this, by leaving two colonists with the Indians in the uncomfortable situation of hostages, a rather usual custom. Philip then decided it would be safe for him to confer with the colonists, whereupon with some of his men he approached Crossman's Hill, on the outskirts of Taunton. Here he again became suspicious, and well he might have felt so, because some of the Plymouth contingent wanted to attack him then and there, but were restrained from doing so by the more prudent representatives of the Bay Colony. He was finally persuaded by the Massachusetts men to attend the conference provided it were staged in the Meeting House and provided also that he and his warriors were stationed on one side of the church while the colonists should occupy the other side. This interesting scene is depicted in a painting owned by the New England Mutual Life Insurance Company and reproduced in this booklet.

At the conference it was proved pretty conclusively that the Indian Chieftain was arming, and not against the Narragansetts as he declared, but to oppose the colonists. When the English Ambassador asked him why he wanted to make war against them and asked him to make a treaty, he is said to have replied: "Your governor of Massachusetts is but a subject of King Charles of England. I shall not treat with a subject, I shall treat of peace only with the king, my brother; when he comes, I am ready." Mr. Haley, who helped me a great deal in compiling the two Indian booklets, believes that the title of "King" was at this time added to Philip's name. He seemed to be confused, and finally consented to surrender the arms they had with them and to send others later and also to make a treaty of submission, which displeased his captains greatly. It is said that one of them deserted to the English.

The treaty itself is worth noting:

"Taunton, 12th April, 1671"

"Whereas, my father, my brother, and myself, have formerly submitted ourselves and our people unto the king's majesty of England, and to this Colony of New Plymouth, by solemn covenant under our hand, but I having of late, through my indiscretion, and the naughtiness of my heart, violated and broken this my covenant with my friends, by taking up arms with evil intent against them, and that groundlessly; I being now deeply sensible of my unfaithfulness and folly, do desire at this time solemnly to renew my covenant with my ancient friends, and my father's friends above mentioned, and do desire that this may testify to the world against me, if ever I shall again fail in my faithfulness towards them, (whom I have now and at all times found kind to me,) or any other of the English colonies; and as a real pledge of my true intentions, for the future to be faithful and friendly, I do freely engage to resign up to the government of New Plymouth all my English arms, to be kept by them for their security, so long as they shall see reason. For the true performance of the promises, I have hereunto set my hand, together with the rest of my council."

This settlement amounted to little because Philip brought in no more guns, and busied himself in forming alliances with other tribes in preparation for the final great battle that was soon to take place. The Plymouth authorities became again alarmed and summoned the Indian Chief to appear before them about the middle of September. This request met with a refusal. The New England Mutual Life Insurance Company described the situation in one of their booklets issued in 1900:

"He was angry with the English; they had possession of his heritage, his hunting and fishing-grounds; he was necessitated to go elsewhere for the support of his fast-decreasing tribe, and nothing would offset the injuries of his race but the utter extermination of the hated English."

Secretary Morton of the Plymouth Government told the authorities of Massachusetts that they were on the point of proceeding against him and desired the assistance of the Bay Colony. Either by chance, or by intuition, Philip surprised both governments by coming to Boston at the same time that this word arrived in Boston. Philip appealed to Massachusetts against the threats of Plymouth, and it was arranged to have his case arbitrated, more fully described in the first chapter.

Francis Baylies, in summing up Philip's career, said this, "Though the sachem of a petty tribe, he raised himself to a prouder eminence than was ever attained by any of the aboriginal race in North America."

NATICK AND NONANTUM

A traveler from across the water, John Dunton, "Late Citizen of London," where he was a book-seller, spent a few months in America during the year 1685 to collect a debt and sell some books. While in Boston he made many friends, and among other things visited Natick. His description of his journey and reception there is interesting and amusing, and it might be well to begin this chapter with his account of the trip. He first speaks of a Widow Brick (probably Breck) who "is a Gentlewoman whose Head (*i.e.,* her Husband) has been cut off, and yet she lives and Walks: But don't be frighted, for she's Flesh and Blood Still, and perhaps some of the *Finest* that you ever saw. . . . The next is Mrs. T . . . whose Tongue runs around like a Wheel, one spoke after another, for there's no end on't; She makes more Noise and jangling than the Bells do on a Coronation Day." Then he goes on to say, "My next Ramble was to Roxbury, in order to Visit the Reverend Mr. Eliot, the great apostle of the Indians. He was pleas'd to receive me with Abundance of Respect; . . . and presented me with Twelve Indian Bibles."

Dunton decided to take Widow Brick with him on this visit, but was evidently sorry he had done so.

"I was glad of the Opportunity to acquaint my self with the Manners, Religion and Government of the Indians. When we were setting forward, I was forc'd out of Civility and Gratitude, to take Madam Brick behind me on Horse-Back; 'tis true, she was the flower of Boston, but in this Case, prov'd no more than a Beautiful sort of Luggage to me. We had about Twenty Miles to Natick, where the best Accommodations we cou'd meet with, were very course. We ty'd up our Horses in two old Barns, that were almost laid in Ruines, however we cou'd discern where they had stood formerly. But there was no place where we cou'd bestow our selves, unless, upon the Greenswerd, till the Lecture began. The Wigwams, or Indian Houses are no more than so many Tents."

From "Nonantum and Natick" by Sarah S. Jacobs

CHRISTIAN, OR PRAYING, INDIANS BUILDING THE FIRST CHURCH IN SOUTH NATICK, MASSACHUSETTS
At the time of the formation of this Indian settlement, in 1651. The exact location was along the Charles River near Eliot Bridge on Pleasant Street. Waban was the first Indian convert, his successor being Daniel Takawampait, whose grave is near by.

Of his reception by the Indians at Natick, now South Natick, and of his return journey he wrote:

"While we were making such Discoveries as these, we were inform'd that the SACHIM, or the Indian King, and his Queen, were there. The Place, 'tis true, did not look like the Royal Residence, however we cou'd easily believe the Report, and went immediately to visit their King and Queen; and here my Courage did not fail as when I wanted my Ruffles, for I stept up and kiss'd the Indian Queen; making her two very low Bows, which she return'd very civilly. The Sachim was very tall, and well limb'd, but had no Beard, and a sort of a Horse Face. The Queen was well shap'd, and her Features might pass pretty well, she had Eyes as Black as Jet, and Teeth as white as Ivory; her Hair was very black and long, and she was considerably up in Years; . . .

Kindness of J. C. Allen

JOHN ELIOT MEMORIAL TERRACE AT NONANTUM (NOW NEWTON), MASSACHUSETTS

At this settlement were established the first civil laws in this country for the regulation of the aborigines. The inscription reads, "Here at Nonantum, October 28, 1646, in Waban's wigwam, near this spot John Eliot began to preach the Gospel to the Indians. Here he founded the first Christian community of Indians within the English Colonies." It is situated on Eliot Memorial Road, which leads off Waverly Avenue, almost a continuation of Grant Avenue, leading from Commonwealth Avenue.

"When we had made our Visit to the Indian King and Queen, we went to the Meeting-Place where the Lecture was Preach'd by Mr. Gookin. . . .

"The Natick-Lecture was done about Four in the Afternoon, and we had Twenty Miles to Boston, so that we were oblig'd to mount immediately, and make the best of our way.

"We had rid but a few Miles, till Mr. Cook, with Madam Middleton behind him, gave us the Slip, . . .

"Shortly after, the Beautiful and Religious Madam Brick, and my self, were very warmly engag'd in Discourse, and so lost both our way, and the sight of our Company; and one Misfortune led on to another, for we found our selves among Bogs, and encompass'd with desperate Precipices; however, we wander'd as chearfully as the Circumstances wou'd admit, for the World can scarce furnish a Companion more agreeable than Madam Brick — This Lady had more Charms than ever Calypso wore, when she kept Ulysses Prisoner in the Chains of Love."

While there the visitors tied their horse in a barn, this word serving as a reminder of a remark made by one of the whites, "O! Lord, I have heard of thy house; but now mine eyes have seen thy Barn," thereby offending the Indians very much.

At Natick was the Indian settlement, but previous to that John Eliot organized a temporary home at Nonantum, meaning "Rejoicing," now in the eastern part of Newton, then part of Cambridge Village and near Watertown Mill on the south side of Charles River. The General Court supplied the land. Here on Nonantum Hill the Apostle first preached to the Indians in their language, and here was a cluster of wigwams over

ANOTHER VIEW OF THE JOHN ELIOT MEMORIAL TERRACE AT NONANTUM, NOW NEWTON

From a picture loaned by Chester H. Phillips
JOHN ELIOT PREACHING TO THE INDIANS

which Waban, the first convert, mentioned later, was chief. In 1879 there was erected an attractive and quite elaborate terrace, shown in an illustration, and the inscription by President Eliot reads, "Here at Nonantum, October 28, 1646, in Waban's wigwam, near this spot, John Eliot began to preach the Gospel to the Indians. Here was founded the first Christian community of Indians within the English Colonies." On the front appear the names of Eliot's associate missionaries, Heath, Shepard, Gookin, Waban. The location is a difficult one to find as it is at the end of a blind street called Eliot Memorial Road which leads off Waverly Avenue, almost a continuation of Grant Avenue, leading off Commonwealth Avenue. The terrace overlooks the Commonwealth Country Club Golf Links, but probably few of the golfers realize its significance.

This first visit there in October of 1646 is well described by Convers Francis in his Life of John Eliot:

"Mr. Eliot in company with three others, whose names are not mentioned, having implored the divine blessing on the undertaking, made his first visit to the Indians on the 28th of October, 1646, at a place afterwards called Nonantum, a spot, that has the honor of being the first, on which a civilized and Christian settlement of Indians was effected within the English colonies of North America. This name was given to the high grounds in the northeast part of Newton, and to the bounds of that town and Watertown. At a short distance from the wigwams, they were met by Waban, a leading man among the Indians at that place. . . .

Some difficult questions were put up to Eliot and the other teachers such as: "Whether the Lord could understand prayers in Indian" and "How all the world became full of people, if they were all once

From a photograph
MONUMENT TO JOHN ELIOT IN THE
BACON FREE LIBRARY GROUNDS
AT SOUTH NATICK
Located at the old Indian Cemetery.

drowned in the flood." Another one wished to have it explained to him why salt water was salt and fresh water fresh. Still another questioner asked, "Why did not God kill the Devil, that made all men so bad, God having all the power?" It would be interesting to know what the answers were. On one of Eliot's visits to a distant "Praying Town" he was asked the r a t h e r embarrassing question, "why those who prayed among the English loved the Indians that prayed to God, more than their own brethren." It is said that the minister avoided a direct reply by reciting several quotations from the Scriptures. At one of these meetings Eliot declared that none of the Indians slept during the sermon.

At the Nonantum settlement were established the first civil laws in this country for the regulation of the aborigines. Much care was taken to instruct the men and women in some trade, and it is said the latter learned to spin quite well. Besides Eliot, Rev. Mr. Wilson, Gookin, Governor Bradford, Deputy Governor Thomas Dudley, and Governor Endicott of

Salem, President Dunster of Harvard, and Rev. Mr. Allen of Dedham attended lectures at Nonantum. On one occasion an Indian woman inquired whether her husband's prayers signified anything, adding that before her husband prayed he used to get very angry, that since he had begun to pray, "he was not angry so much, but only a little angry." A male made the complaint that "If we Indians get drunk, we are severely whipped, but if the English get drunk, they merely go and sleep it off, or perhaps have to pay a slight fine."

John Eliot, after continuing the settlement of Nonantum for five years, came to the conclusion in the spring of 1651 that he

From a photograph.
OLD GRAVESTONE OF DANIEL
TAKAWAMPAIT, SOUTH NATICK,
MASSACHUSETTS
Placed in the wall running along Pleasant Street. Takawampait succeeded John Eliot in this Indian settlement.

preferred to have one farther away from the whites, as some "exerted a pernicious influence upon them." He rode on horseback in search of a suitable location, and finally a friendly Indian suggested a situation which was named Natick, "place of hills," and now known as South Natick, "in the wilderness," as a writer expressed it. The wigwams, provisions and other possessions were transported up the Charles River, and on Eliot Plain near Eliot Bridge near the corner of Union and Pleasant Streets the town was laid out. It is of interest to know that Dedham exchanged six thousand acres here for the township of Deerfield, but for what reason it is difficult to see. Later on Waban's son attended school at Dedham. A foot bridge was built

From a photograph
CLOSE VIEW OF GRAVESTONE OF
DANIEL TAKAWAMPAIT
The wording is: "Here Lyes the Body of
Daniel Takawampait. Aged 64 years.
Died September the 17th, 1716."

by the Indians at the location of the present Eliot Bridge. The town was laid out in three streets, two on the north side of the river and one on the south, with house lots for every family. Most of this property belonged to an Indian called John Speen, who signed a quit-claim deed made out in Eliot's handwriting and now in the Bacon Library situated on the field where the graveyard stood. The grantor of the land was allotted lands there as part of the agreement. The next step was to form a government, one ruler over a hundred persons, two rulers over each fifty, and then each group chose one of their members out of each ten. A building was erected by the newcomers, fifty by twenty-five feet, and two stories high, the lower floor to serve as a sanctuary on Sundays and a schoolroom on weekdays, the upper story serving as a warehouse.

Waban, meaning "The Wind," was the first Indian convert; he was an efficient ruler of fifty and also constable in this Natick town. He is described by Gookin as "a person of great presidence and piety: I do not know any Indian that excels him." There are several stories told about him. He issued a warrant on one occasion, worded: "You, you big constable, quick you catch um Jeremiah off scow, strong you hold um, safe you bring um, afore me, Waban, justice peace." At another time he was asked what he would do if he found an Indian drunk: "Tie um all up, and whip um plaintiff, and whip um fendant, and whip um witness." Waban was sent to Deer Island in 1675 and died about 1677. A well-known lake not far from his settlement bears his name.

Eliot's successor at Natick was Daniel Takawampait, who was ordained a teacher there about 1687. Eliot called him "a person of

ELIOT CHURCH AND REMAINS OF THE OLD ELIOT OAK (REMOVED IN 1936), UNDER WHICH JOHN ELIOT PREACHED TO THE INDIANS, AT SOUTH NATICK, MASSACHUSETTS

A tablet to his memory is set into the boulder seen in the picture.

good knowledge." His memory and work performed here have been carefully preserved by an old headstone which is placed in the stone wall on his grave on Pleasant Street, which bisects the ancient settlement, and runs up the hill towards the Unitarian Church, where Eliot first preached to the Indians. Takawampait died in 1716. Rev. Mr. Wilson of the First Church in Boston wrote of his visit to Natick with Governor Endicott:

"The Governor came with about 20 horsemen from Dedham, and made a like view, after which there was a lecture or sermon in the fort, which the Indians have made of whole trees, very handsome and firm, which is near a fair house which the Indians have built after the English manner, high and large, without assistance (except of an English carpenter a day or two to direct, about the time of raising)

Photographed through kindness of Superintendent of Buildings Kimball

MURAL ON WALL OF MEMORIAL HALL, STATE HOUSE, BOSTON, SHOWING ELIOT PREACHING TO THE INDIANS

From "Lives of Famous Indian Chiefs" by
Norman B. Wood
Published by American Indian Historical Pub-
lishing Co., Brady Block, Aurora, Ill.
Copyrighted in 1906 by American Indian His-
torical Publishing Co.

KING PHILIP REJECTING ELIOT'S
PREACHING
The Chieftain is said to have remarked:
"Why should I give up my thirty-seven
gods for your one?"

with chimneys in it. . . ." The Governor wrote: "The Meeting house was fifty feet long, twenty-five broad, well sawed and framed, the enclosure without the fort, about a quarter of an acre."

Several stories of the settlement might well be introduced here. A Natick Indian, named Ephraim, was asked why young Indians educated by the English often became drunk, although they had behaved well when in charge of the colonists. His reply was, "Tucks (ducks) will be tucks, for all ole hen he hatchum." Another anecdote is told of another Indian of Natick who journeyed to Boston with a load of brooms and baskets and while there purchased a dram of liquor. On a visit there some months later the same storekeeper charged him twice as much for the same quantity. The Indian quite naturally asked the reason for the increase, whereupon the dealer informed him that he had stored the wine all winter, which was as expensive as to keep a horse. "Hah!" said the Indian, "he no eat as much hay, but he drink as much water."

Oliver Peabody was appointed in 1721 to teach the Indians at Natick, and helped Takawampait very much. Once, while praying for rain, he made use of the Biblical formula, "May the bottles of heaven be unstopped and a plentiful supply of rain be poured down on the thirsty earth." Rain did follow and continued for some days, whereupon one of his Indian congregation observed: "I believe them are bottles you talked about be unstopped, and the stopples be lost."

The Indians planted "Friendship Trees" in front of the houses of the early ministers. The last of six stanzas written by Maria Butler and dedicated to these trees, reads:

"And so, of all historic trees
Made famous long ago
None were so sacred, quite, as these
That Red Men did bestow;
For Gratitude had planted them,
And Love had made them grow."

Of course there were some surprisingly strict regulations, several of which are repeated: If any man shall beat his wife, his hands shall be tied behind him. If any woman shall not have her hair tied up, but hang loose, or be cut as men's hair, she shall pay five shillings. All men that wear long locks shall pay five shillings. If any shall kill their lice between their teeth, they shall pay five shillings.

From "The History of Woodstock, Connecticut," by Clarence Winthrop Bowen, Ph.D., LL.D.
Privately printed by The Plimpton Press, Norwood, Mass., 1926
JOHN ELIOT, 1604–1690
Graduate of Jesus College, University of Cambridge, England, 1622. Visited Woodstock September 15 and 16, 1674. From a reputed portrait owned by the Museum of Fine Arts, Boston.

John Eliot was learned, conscientious, a hard worker and generous. His chief interest, of course, was to educate and Christianize the Indians and in this respect he would have been more successful had not King Philip's War taken place. Mather also called attention to the fact that Eliot's name spelled reversed reads "toile." In a letter to Governor Winslow, the "Apostle" wrote, "I have not been dry, night or day, from the third day of the week till the sixth, but so travel, and at night pull off my boots, wring my stockings, and put them on again, and so continue."

An example of his generosity was explained by Oliver Bacon in his history of Natick:

"So great was his charity that his salary was often distributed for the relief of his needy neighbors so soon after the period at which he received it, that before another period arrived his own family were straitened for the comforts of life. One day the parish treasurer, on paying him the money for salary due, which he put into a handkerchief, in order to prevent Mr. E. from giving away his money before he got home, tied the ends into as many hard knots as he could. The good man received his handkerchief and took leave of the treasurer. He immediately went to the house of a sick family. . . . Eliot with moistened eyes began to untie the knots. After many efforts to get at his money, and impatient at the delay and perplexity, he threw his handkerchief, money and all, into the lap of the mother. . . ."

As Eliot approached old age he used to say that he was afraid some of his friends, who had died, especially John Cotton and Richard Mather, would suspect him to have gone the wrong way, because he had remained so long after them.

The pervading spirit of the times is shown in these amusing stanzas:

"When plucked geese are mutton,
And slaughtered sow is veal,
I'll meet you and your Indians,
And have a princely meal.

When six and eight make ten,
And four and seven are nine,
Then call your Indians together again,
And I'll be there to dine."

His  mark,

Waban.

*From "Nonantum and Natick" by Sarah S. Jacobs, Boston
Massachusetts Sabbath School Society.
Entered according to Act of Congress 1853 by Christopher C. Dean, District Court of District
of Massachusetts*

INDIAN SIGNATURE

INDIANS INTERNED ON DEER ISLAND

Deer Island in Boston Harbor was used as a place of detention as early as October, 1675, when about five hundred Christian, or Praying Indians, were interned there by the colonists shortly after the commencement of King Philip's War, which was to decide whether the English or the Indians were to govern our lands. At its outbreak there were about eleven hundred converts, half of whom were probably not really sincere in their new belief, and they occupied fourteen Praying Towns, as they were called, in Massachusetts. The situation of these Indians, as one can readily see, was very uncertain and insecure, for their compatriots were naturally openly hostile to them and at the same time the colonists to whom they had submitted and whose religion they had adopted were distrustful of them. Furthermore, those Indians who were hostile to the intruders upon their lands endeavored to stir up trouble between their compatriots and the colonists and many false accusations were made. They knew King Philip hated them and so they placed their hopes and reliance upon the English, who were engaged in a life-and-death struggle and who hesitated on the proper course to pursue in regard to their allies. They therefore had the good will of neither side.

When the war began the Indians in the Praying Towns concluded to construct forts for better security and it was suggested that some of the English should be placed there to supervise them, an idea to which the Indians themselves readily acceded. As it turned out, however, only a few redskins left their settlements and joined the army of Philip, and undoubtedly the English should have trusted them more and made greater use of their fighting prowess and knowledge of Indian methods of warfare. The aborigines often said that in action they had the advantage of their enemies in several ways; they themselves in their marches and battles always spread out, whereas the English usually kept "in a heap together," so that it "was as easy to hit them as to hit a house," as they expressed it.

The English soon came to regard the Praying Indians with such suspicion that the General Court passed stringent regulations that none should be allowed to enter any town unless under the guard of two musketeers, and anyone found without such a guard might be arrested. Nevertheless, in spite of this distrust, Daniel Gookin was requested on July 2, 1675, to go to their villages and select one-third of the able-bodied men to join the army at Mount Hope. An Indian Company of fifty-two men was thereupon

MASSACHUSETTS.—THE ZUNI INDIAN CHIEFS CELEBRATING AN ANCIENT RELIGIOUS RITE AT DEER ISLAND, MARCH 29th. FILLING THEIR SACRED VESSELS WITH WATER FROM THE ATLANTIC.—

ZUNI INDIAN CHIEFS FROM NEW MEXICO CELEBRATING AN ANCIENT RELIGIOUS RITE AT DEER ISLAND, IN MARCH, 1882.

quickly raised and conducted there by Captain Isaac Johnson. They did well, but the officers, probably only naturally, were prejudiced against them. The Natick Indians, it is reported, behaved particularly well in one of the first encounters with King Philip, and one wonders at all why they could be persuaded to fight against their own tribesmen. Some of the colonists, however, accused their allies of skulking and of shooting over the heads of the enemy, and although some of them brought four Indian scalps to Governor Leverett as proof of their loyalty, they were still distrusted. In order to satisfy the people the Governor and Council on August 30 passed an order that the Praying Indians must confine themselves to five of their villages, Natick, Hassanamesit, now Grafton; Nashobah, now Littleton; Wamesit, now part of Tewksbury; and Ponkapoag, now included in Stoughton. None were allowed to go more than one mile from the centre of these settlements, which of course proved a great hardship, for it hindered them in their hunting and prevented them from tending their cattle.

John Watson, an Indian Agent, and Captain Henry Prentice of Cambridge, went to Natick to investigate their loyalty, and although the former was much prejudiced against them before his visit, they both testified to the Council that the Indians conducted themselves properly and that they were faithful to the English. Watson was even accused of taking sides against the whites, and their visit was really of little avail. On the same day that the order was issued to keep within their settlements, several English found some Indians in Marlboro gathering corn and promptly sent them to Boston, where they were wrongly tried on a charge of murder and several sold into slavery. The citizens of Boston became much excited and some even wanted the remaining Indians executed. They were, however, released.

About the middle of October the people again made so many complaints that the magistrates appointed a committee which decided that the Indians should be allocated evenly among certain towns nearer the seaboard. The places chosen were Cambridge, Concord, Dorchester, Mendon and Noddle's Island (now East Boston), but of course the residents of these places strenuously objected and refused to allow the plan to be adopted. Moreover, the Indians themselves preferred to remain where they were. When those at the Natick settlement became aware of what was contemplated they sent a petition through John Watson, who had been appointed their guardian, requesting the court to show them due consideration, entreating that body not to listen to any false charges against them. They also suggested that either more Englishmen should be sent to live with them as witnesses of their good behavior, or else that they should hand over some of their leading men to be held as hostages for their good conduct. They furthermore begged not to be taken from their wigwams just as winter was approaching, because it would be such a hardship upon the aged and ill. They also professed innocence and guaranteed their loyalty to the colonists. These proposals seemed extremely fair, but unfortunately several other incidents that took place at that time were laid at the door of the innocent Praying Indians and the colonists became still more incensed. In order to appease them the General Court passed a vote in October that "all the Naticke Indians be forthwith sent for, and disposed of to Deare Island, as the place appointed for their present aboade." It was first of all necessary to get the consent of the owner of the island, Samuel Shrimpton, of Boston, who readily granted permission provided no wood should be cut or any of his sheep killed. Most of the islands in Boston Harbor in the early days were covered with forests and presented a very attractive appearance.

The removal was carried out gently and tactfully by a friendly Englishman named Captain Prentice, with the aid of several others brought by him for that purpose. Upon reaching Natick he told the Indians of the decision of the Magistrates, and in one or two hours they reluctantly packed up their few belongings and quietly though sadly started to carry out the request. Six carts had been provided to convey their possessions and those who were ill or old; and the little band of two hundred men, women and children started forth on their melancholy journey to a place then called "The Pines," near the grounds of the present United States Arsenal at Watertown on the banks of the Charles River, and about two miles above Cambridge. Here in 1630 had been the scene of a meeting between the new arrivals, the Puritans and the Indians, when a friendly exchange was made of a bass for an English biscuit. All the Indians at Natick were brought there with the exception of old Jethro, who with his whole family managed to escape during the night. He himself had been imprisoned in Boston and did not much relish the idea of spending a cold winter on Deer Island. The Indians from Marlboro were surrounded in their fort by Captain Mosely, and their arms seized. They were then taken to Boston, their hands tied behind their backs, and connected by a long cart rope. They met the Naticks on the way and probably were ferried to Deer Island with them.

Reverend John Eliot, of course, did not believe in their removal and with Gookin met them at "The Pines" to console and comfort them. Of their departure from Natick the Roxbury Church Records contain these lines written by the Apostle himself:

"When the Indians were hurried away to an Iland at half an hours warning, pore soules in terror y left theire goods. books. bibles. only some few caryed yr bibles. the rest were spoyled & lost. So yt wⁿ the wares wʳ finishd & y returned to yʳ places, y wʳ greatly impovisht, but y especially bewailed yᵉ want of Bibles. yˢ made me meditate upon a 2ᵈ impʳssion of o Bible. & accordingly tooke pains to revise the first edition. I also intreated mr. John Cotton to help in y work, he having obtained some ability so to doe."

The Indians were very gloomy and disconsolate over the prospect before them and some actually believed they were to be shipped out of the country and perhaps sold into slavery as had been done before in the case of some captives. Many spent their time crying and praying and the scene is described as being very pathetic. It is said that several of the English who were there were much affected by the sight. At high tide about midnight on October 30th they were embarked on three boats and taken down the river and across the Harbor to their internment camps, "patiently, humbly, and piously, without murmuring or complaining against ye English," wrote Eliot. To their numbers were added some Praying Indians from Ponkapoag who were on some slight pretext ordered to the island. Huntoon in his History of Canton states that it was deemed advisable to place all of the tribe under command of Quartermaster Thomas Swift of Milton, who took them to Long Island and when released he removed them to the Brush Hill Camp. A few years later they were ordered to their plantation at Ponkapoag. This was also the case with respect to about fifty-eight Nashobahs, then at the Concord or Musketaquid settlement, who, to quote a history of the town, were to "pass into the furnace of affliction with their brethren and countrymen." All their provisions, including a large crop of corn, had to be abandoned. It has been figured that before winter came there were between four and five hundred on Deer Island. Gookin claims that there was also a large number of friendly Indians and also prisoners encamped on Long Island in our harbor, but their approximate numbers cannot be ascertained. The Records of the Colony of New Plymouth under date of February 29, 1676, stated that, "The councell of warr now assembled doe order, that the Namassachesett Indians be speedily remoued to Clarkes Illand, and ther to remaine, and not to depart from thence without lycence from authoritie vpon paine of death." It was necessary to pass votes regulating the conduct of the prisoners on these islands, and from the "Records of the Governor and Company of the Massachusetts Bay in New England," we find these votes, under date of November 3, 1675: "That none of the sajd Indians shall presume to goe off the sajd islands voluntarily, vpon payne of death; and it shall be laufull for the English to destroy those that they shall finde stragling off from the sajd places of theire confinement, vnless taken of by order from authorjty, and vnder an English guard. And it is further ordered, that if any person or persons shall presume to take, steale, or carry away either man, woeman, or child of the sajd Indians, off from any the sajd islands where they are placed, wthout order from the Generall Court or council, he or they shall be accounted breakers of the capitall law printed and published against man stealing and this order to be forthuith posted and published." The same court voted: "that the country Tresurer take care for ye provision of these Indians that are sent doune to Deare Island, so as to pvent (prevent) their perishing by any extremity that they may be put vnto for want of absolute necessaries, and for that end he is to appoint meet psons to vissit them from time to time."

As may readily be expected, their sufferings during the winter were very severe, for their rude shelters were inadequate, their clothing scanty and their food, consisting chiefly of shell-fish and clams, was unhealthy and also insufficient, in spite of almost continuous fishing and digging. They nevertheless were protected from the rage of the people. Many of course died, but they uttered few complaints and we hear of no attempts on their part to swim the Gut. During the early part of the following year, on account of "the present distressed condition of the Indians at the Island, they being ready to perish for want of bread, and incapacitated to make provision for the future," it was ordered that "there be a man wth a boate provided, who, wth some of the Indians, shall be imployed in catching of fish."

John Eliot and Daniel Gookin often visited Deer Island and doubtless other islands to comfort the prisoners and to look after their wants. The interest these two men took in the Indians caused the populace to denounce them severely and the life of the latter was even threatened.

During these months of confinement in the harbor King Philip was successful in his warfare and many disasters befell the English settlements, the most serious being the massacre of Deerfield, during which Captain Samuel Mosely distinguished himself for his bravery. It will be remembered that it was his custom to hang his wig on a tree when a fight seemed imminent, which caused the enemy to remark that he was a man with two heads, and therefore twice as hard to kill. It was during this onslaught, when with a handful of men he was attacked by a much greater band of Indians, that his antagonists yelled to him, "Come, Mosely, come; you seek Indians, you want Indians, here is Indians enough for you." The assault on Medfield followed some months afterwards, on February 21st, whereupon the Bostonians became greatly excited, and to quote Gookin, cried out, "Oh, come, let us go down to Deer Island, and kill all the praying Indians." He adds, "They could not come at the enemy Indians, for they were too crafty and subtle for the English; therefore they would have wreaked their rage upon the poor unarmed Indians our friends, (had not the authority of the country restrained them;) for about this time the Council was informed by good testimony, that about thirty or forty men were entering into a combination, to convey themselves out to the Island, at Pulling Point, the narrowest place between it and the main, and to have cut off all the poor Christian Indians." The Council fortunately found several of the ringleaders and made them give up the idea. Some of the citizens, nevertheless, still persisted in having them deported. Finally the saner ones learned that five of the leaders, who had submitted to the English at Court some years previously, were on Deer Island, and this fact seemed to turn the tide in their favor, and to calm the excited populace.

The Council at Boston now thought it advisable to learn more of the whereabouts of the enemy and asked Gookin to consider the problem. After deliberating with some of those on the island, he chose Job Kattenanet of Natick and James Quanapohit for this difficult task, the reward to be five pounds apiece. These two Indian spies spent the night in secret at Gookin's house and before daybreak on December 30th they started out on their mission. After an absence of three weeks James returned to the home of Isaac Williams at the Falls of the Charles. He had walked eighty miles through deep snow and arrived exhausted. He then reported to Gookin and the Council that he had met the enemy beyond Lancaster, and under the pretense of getting information for their friends on Deer Island, he learned considerable news, including the intended attack upon Lancaster. James escaped with the aid of a friend, but Job remained in search of his children, who had fallen into the hands of the enemy. These two spies were obliged to return to their prison camp in spite of the valuable service they had rendered. In fact, the popular opinion was still so against them that they were accused of bringing in false information. Job was not allowed to keep an engagement that might have brought him back his children and consequently he worried much in his island habitation.

The war still continued and the colonists found it necessary in their extremity to make still further use of the interned Indians on Deer Island. The General Court voted on February 1676 to raise an army of six hundred men and Major Savage was chosen Commander-in-Chief. He refused, however, to accept the undertaking unless he would be allowed to employ the island Indians to help him. It was decided that Captain John Curtice (Curtis) of Roxbury be "impowered to take sixe Indians from the island for his assistance, wth their armes, some of wch Indians may be improoved for spies as the commander in chief shall appoint." He chose six braves, including the same Job and James, who already had shown their good qualities. They were very cheerful at being chosen. While on the march through Marlboro Job searched for his three children again, and they were finally delivered to Captain Thomas Savage, who sent them to Boston, and from there to Deer Island, where the family was again united. The next turn in affairs was the suggestion made to the Council by Captain Henchman, who had been chosen to look after the interned Indians. He urged the magistrates to permit him to lead a small company against the enemy, explaining that the children and relatives left on the island would be ample security for their loyalty. His recommendation at first was not accepted, but later, towards the end of April, the Council voted to arm and send out a Company of seventy men under Captain Samuel Hunting and Lieutenant James Richardson, who knew the Indians well. Arms could be procured for only forty, and after the men were selected they set out on April 21st for Charlestown on their way to Chelmsford. They learned of the attack on Sudbury and marched to that town, where they performed good service, although arriving too late to prevent the disaster to Captain Wadsworth and his troops. These Christian soldiers were employed on all expeditions while the war lasted, and new recruits were added to the ranks as arms continued to arrive from England, until finally by the time summer came their numbers were doubled.

The sufferings of the four hundred or so older men, and of the women and children who were left on the islands continued, although spring with its warmer weather had already arrived. Fortunately the excellent record of their fighting men caused the English to relent and in May the General Court passed an order for their removal to the mainland provided they would do so at their own expense. Gookin by authority of the Corporation in London and the General Court here, came again to their assistance and hired boats for their transportation to Cambridge. They were then taken care of by Thomas Oliver who resided near Charles River, which afforded them a convenient place for fishing. There was also a fortification near their wigwams to which they could retire should they be attacked. This change was a most welcome one, especially as some of their number were ill at the time, including Waban, who, before the war, was the leading Christian and Justice of the Peace at Natick. Gookin and Eliot, as in many other instances, provided the sick ones with food and medicine and all recovered. Most of them, with the exception of a few who helped the English get in their harvests, remained on Oliver's estate all that summer. The Ponkapoag Indians were placed in a fort on Brush Hill, Milton, the location of which is not known.

The war was now nearing its end and the help of the Indian allies and Christian Indians contributed much towards bringing it to a conclusion. The colonists had suffered the loss of about six hundred of their best men, thirteen towns had been destroyed, and six hundred dwellings laid low. In fact, about one-eleventh of their resources were gone, but these figures would have been much more serious had it not been for their Indian converts, who, through their knowledge of the country and the mode of warfare, were able to render such valuable services. Their own losses testify to their usefulness. The war was a sad blow to the cause of Christianity among the natives, for many of them seemed to disappear or desert, chiefly from the newer Praying Towns; some became heathen again, some were killed in the conflict, some died on the islands during captivity and were buried there, some proved untrustworthy and were executed as rebels, and some died of starvation. A few were later united with the English. Eliot, however, continued to be as helpful as possible and endeavored to follow their careers, even of those who unfortunately were sold into slavery as far away as Africa.

Several authorities have estimated that four hundred of the Indian Allies were either captured or killed, and it has been said that they actually killed over three hundred of their countrymen. Their fidelity to the English is rather to be marvelled at, particularly when one considers they were pitted against their own kind. There are some interesting testimonials that were made by some of the English officers serving over them. Captain Daniel Henchman reported that at Deer Island, and on the Mount Hope and other expeditions, he had "experience of the sobriety, courage, and fidelity of the generality of these Indians." Captain Samuel Hunting said that the Indian Company of eighty men in one year "behaved themselves courageously and faithfully to the English interest." Thomas Savage certified under date of December 20, 1677, that the Christian Indians under him "carried themselves well, and proved themselves courageous soldiers, and faithful to the English interest." Gookin himself wrote that they "may be judged to have no small share in the effects and consequences of this war."

HARVARD AND THE INDIAN

At the exercises in 1904 attending the laying of the cornerstone of the new Dartmouth Hall of Dartmouth College, an institution that was originally founded for the education of the Indian, the late President Eliot of Harvard University surprised the audience by referring in these words to the connection between his University and the Indian:

"Moreover, in the early generations in New England it was not only English scholarship, but English benevolence, which developed the first schools and colleges among us. And it is an interesting fact to recall . . . that the origin of Harvard College was partly similar in motive and purpose to the origin of Dartmouth. . . . You have heard during this festivity that it was for Indians that Dartmouth College was originally founded. That is in part true of Harvard also. In the charter of 1650 given by the Colony it is expressly declared that the President and Fellows of Harvard College are to take care for the education of English and Indian youth. Moreover, it was English benevolence which built at Harvard the first Indian college. To be sure, they were never able to fill that building with Indian students, and it soon passed into other uses; but there is the fact — a fact of the seventeenth century, one hundred years before the Dartmouth experience — that English benevolence set the example of charitable educational aid for the Indian race."

President Eliot included in his address the facetious remark made by Oliver Wendell Holmes, who often told his friends that he held so many positions at Cambridge that he occupied not a chair but a settee.

As early as 1635 a Londoner, Dr. John Stoughton, showed a philanthropic interest in the Indians of Massachusetts and even suggested building a college here in which to instruct them. Nothing, however, came of the idea. Harvard's first President, Henry Dunster, at an early date showed a good deal of interest in educating the natives, and in 1645 John Eliot sent to him a pair of "hopeful young plants" upon which to try his skill in teaching. His rather curious expense account for fourteen months has been recorded:

"For the Diet and washing of the two Indians since the 3rd of the 8th month hitherto, considering the attendance of the younger, being a very childe, what you think meet — 16 pounds." Then followed an item for "Physick for James during his sickness" and others for "making them 12 bands and 8 shirts" and "for buttons, thred and other materials." A year or so later John Eliot notified the Indians that if enough of them congregated in Cambridge during the meeting to be held there on June 9th, 1647 he would be glad to preach to them. Morison has described this occasion very well:

"Before the meeting John Eliot, who had a sound showman's instinct, let it be known among the Indians that if they attended in sufficient numbers he would preach to them and in all the long history of the College Yard there has been no more picturesque scene than on that June afternoon. The reverend elders in their black doublets and white bands, the worshipful magistrates in their impressive cloaks, sundry townspeople, and such students as had not been turned out to make room for delegates, in their brighter and more varied costumes, were grouped about the steps of the Old College. John Eliot takes his place in the centre; and about him, eagerly drinking in his words, squat the 'heathen' in all their unspoiled dirt and color. The sermon over, Indians propound questions, such as

What Countrey man Christ was, and where he was borne?
How farre off that place was from us here?
Where Christ now was?
How they might lay hold on him, and where, being now absent from them?

And when these are answered, and the Indians have professed themselves satisfied by their accustomed grunts, John Eliot tries out his catechism on 'divers poore naked children,' who shrill out the answers in unison."

Thomas Shepard in his book "The Cleare Sun-shine of the Gospel — Breaking Forth Upon The Indians in New England" gives this version of this meeting:

"There is one thing more which I would acquaint you with, which hapned this Summer, viz. June 9. the first day of the Synods meeting at Cambridge. . . . the afternoon was spent in hearing an Indian Lecture where there was a great confluence of Indians (from) all parts to heare Mr. Eliot, which we conceived not unseasonable at such a time. . . ."

Few Harvard alumni realize that in this early charter of 1650 it is expressly set forth that the college was organized "for all accommodacons of Buildings and all other necessary prouisions that may conduce to the education of the English and Indian Youth of this Country in knowledge and godlines." The friends of the aborigines believing in their education and Christianization appealed to the Commissioners of the United Colonies, who had charge of the funds raised in London by a society with a very long name. After some correspondence this English society, in September, 1653, proposed to erect at Harvard College, as expressed in Plymouth County Records, "the bjilding of one Intyre Rome (Room) att the College for the Conveniencye of six hopfull Indians youthes to bee trained vp there . . . which Rome may be two storyes high and built plaine but strong and durable." The College was authorized to erect such a building at a

65

cost not exceeding 120 pounds, "besides glasse." President Dunster, who was a firm believer in the education of the Indian, petitioned for a larger building and received permission to erect one. It was left to the Commissioners "to giue order for the finishing of the building att the College and to alter the forme agreed vpon att the last meeting att Boston provided it exceed not thirty foot in length and twenty in breadth." This structure, erected in 1655, of brick, to "exceed not thirty foot in length and twenty in breadth," was large enough to receive about twenty scholars with lodgings and studies and cost between three and four hundred pounds. It was known as the Indian College, but no picture of it has come down to us. It is not mentioned by name in the inventory of December 10, 1654, but the fourth entry, "One small house unfinished, intended for a printing office" doubtless refers to this building. This English Company called "The President and Society for Propagation of the Gospel in New England," known usually as the "New England Company," contributed most of the funds for this building which was to educate Indians to become teachers, ministers and magistrates. As George E. Ellis, a writer on the Indian, well expressed it, "The flavor and restlessness of a forest life were to be extracted from their blood and fibres by a classical and scholarly academic training." He refers to this structure as the first substantial building on the grounds of the college.

It is probable that only six or eight Indians ever attended this school, which was used so little that in 1656 President Chauncy was permitted to improve the structure for the use of English students. This situation is amusingly expressed by Alexander V. Blake in his "Anecdotes of the American Indians": ". . . and now he wished to give them a polite education, that must have sat as gracefully on them as the full-sleeved gown and bands of the divine. Considerable sums were expended in their board and education: . . . It must have been Spartan discipline to the heads as well as hearts of the poor Indians, to labour morn and night through the Greek and Roman authors, to try to discover and relish the beauties of style and the splendour of imagery. No doubt, their thoughts sometimes fled away to their deserts, where their fathers roved in dignity and freedom, and books never came. The design might be praiseworthy, but Providence did not smile upon it; most of these young men died when they had made great proficiency in their studies, as if the languages wore out their hearts; others abandoned their books, even when they were prepared to enter Harvard College, in the town of Cambridge; their patience was probably exhausted, and the boon of literary dignity could lure them no further. A few of these, passing from one extreme to the other, burst their bonds at once, and as if mind and body panted together to be free, hastened back to the wilderness again, into its wigwams and swamps; where neither Homer nor Ovid was like to follow them."

"These circumstances proved very discouraging to the godly in New England," says a contemporary. "Some were so far affected by them as to conceive that they were manifest tokens of the Divine disapprobation. In consequence of the death and failure of those who entered the aforesaid building, it was soon after chiefly occupied by the English."

Several descriptions of this Indian building have been handed down to us. In 1665, Colonel George Cartwright, one of the Royal Commissioners wrote sarcastically: "At Cambridg they haue a small colledg, (made of wood) for the English; and a small brick pile for the Indians, where there was but one; one was lately dead, & 3, or 4 more they had at schole, as they sayd. It may be feared that this college may furnish as many scismaticks to the Church, and the Corporation as many rebelles to the King, as formerly they haue donne, if not timely prevented." Daniel Gookin in 1674 gives the best description: "One thing falls in here fitly to be spoken of, as a means intended for the good of the Indians; which was the erecting of a house of brick at Cambridge in New-England, which passeth under the name of the Indian college. It is a structure strong and substantial, though not very capacious. It cost between three and four hundred pounds. It is large enough to receive and accommodate about twenty scholars with convenient lodgings and studies; but not hitherto hath been improved for the ends intended, by reason of the death and failing of Indian scholars. It hath hitherto been principally improved for to accommodate English scholars, and for placing and using a printing press belonging to the college. This house was built and finished at the charge, and by the appointment, of the Honorable Corporation for propagating the gospel in New-England." Some years later, in 1676, Randolph reported to the Privy Council that the "small brick building, where some Indians did study but now converted to a printing house," was still standing although no longer used as a dormitory. Four years later two Dutchmen, Danckaerts and Sluyter, visited Cambridge and on their return to Holland reported that they "passed by the printing office, but there was nobody in it; the paper sash, however, being broken, we looked in, and saw two presses with six or eight cases of type. There is not much work done there."

On November 6, 1693, the Corporation voted "That ye Jndian Colledge be taken down, provided the Charges of taking it down amount not to more than five pounds." There was no one who was willing to undertake the work at this figure. Cotton Mather was one of those present at this meeting. On September 19, 1695 the Commissioners for "Propagating the Gospel among the Indians" took action that the bricks belonging to the Indian building which "is gone to decay & become altogether Uselesse" be removed and used to make an additional building for Harvard College — and gave their consent provided "that in case any Jndians should hereafter be sent to ye Colledge, they should enjoy their Studies rent free in said building." Stoughton was then being considered. On April 7, 1698, the Corporation passed another vote "that the Bricks of ye old Jndian Colledg be sold to Mr. Willis, he allowing for them 20" (Pounds), and in the following month Sewall wrote: "In the beginning of this Moneth of May, the old Brick Colledge, comonly called the Indian Colledge, is pull'd down to the ground, being sold to Mr. Willis the builder of Mr. Stoughtons colledge." The proceeds were used to pay for the cellar under the southerly end of the first Stoughton Hall.

The Indian structure, now no longer, was not the first Harvard building, but it remained standing for nearly forty-four years, a longer time than the other two known as the "First Colledge" and Goffe,

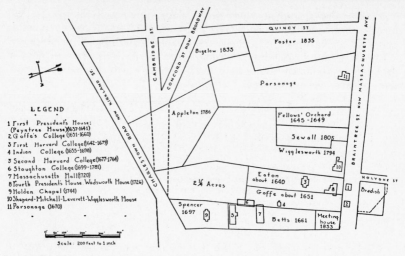

LEGEND

1 First President's House:
(Peyntree House)(1637-1641)
2 Goffe's College (1651-1660)
3 First Harvard College(1642-1679)
4 Indian College (1655-1698)
5 Second Harvard College(1677-1764)
6 Stoughton College(1699-1781)
7 Massachusetts Hall(1720)
8 Fourth President's House Wadsworth House(1726)
9 Holden Chapel (1744)
10 Shepard-Mitchell-Leverett-Wigglesworth House
11 Parsonage (1670)

Scale: 200 feet to 1 inch

From "Publications of the Colonial Society of Massachusetts," Volume XV
PLAN OF HARVARD UNIVERSITY YARD SHOWING THE LOCATION OF THE
INDIAN COLLEGE AT NO. 4 IN THE GOFFE LOT

existed. Nevertheless, curiously enough, its exact location has never
been determined. The late President Eliot in the year 1848 placed
it a trifle north of Wadsworth House, on the Eaton Lot, as it has been
called, and probably within the limits of the present Grays. The
diagram made by Albert Mathews for the Colonial Society is shown
herewith. It is possible that the "First Colledge" building itself was
situated here. The other opinion is based on the fact that some old
bricks were discovered when the cellar of Matthews Hall was exca-
vated. This idea would locate the Indian structure on the Goffe lot
within the limits of and at right angles to Matthews, which lot ran
parallel to the Eaton tract, both being very near Braintree Street, now
Massachusetts Avenue. This latter road formed the southern bound-
ary of what was known by the curious name of Ox Pasture.

Although rather out of place it may be amusing to recall two Harvard regulations of the seventeenth century. Should any undergraduate be absent from his chambers after nine o'clock in the evening
(without sufficient excuse) he was subject to a fine not exceeding two
shillings to be imposed by the President or any of the Tutors. Another rule passed by the Corporation in 1693 was as follows: "The
Corporation haveing been informed that ye Custom taken up in the
Colledge, not used in any other Universities, for the Comencers to
have Plumb-Cake, is dishonourable to ye Colledge, not gratefull to
Wise men, and chargable to ye Parents of ye Comencers; do there-
for(e) put an End to that Custom, and do hereby order that no Com-
mencer or other Scholar shall have any Such Cakes in their Studies
or Chambers, and that if any Scholar shall offend therin, ye Cakes
Shall be taken from him, and he shall moreover pay to the Colledge
twenty shillings for each Such offen(ce)." We also learn that in
the early days of the College there was so little money in the Colony
that wampum, the money of the Indians, was made by law legal

tender for debts, and at times the College steward, as he was called, found it necessary to accept live stock, grain, groceries, and even solids and fluids of various kinds in payment of the term bills of the students.

Some months ago the *Harvard Graduates' Magazine* printed a droll poem about the old pump near Hollis, which, although equally out of place, we reproduce:

> Your wooden arm you hold outstretched
> To shake with passers-by;
> Your friends are always thirsty ones;
>   But you are never dry.
> A hundred Classes at your lips
>   Have drunk, and passed away,
> And where their fathers quenched their thirst
>   The sons now quench to-day.
> Some long for claret or champagne,
>   And some for sherries pale,
> And some indulge in Adam's beer,
>   But you in Adam's ale.

We know very little about the few Indians who found their way to Harvard. We do know that many of the aborigines who were brought into civilization, and were obliged to live amidst new surroundings, died of consumption and that there was a high rate of mortality among those who became scholars. Sickness hindered the teaching of the Indian youths, and undoubtedly this was the reason that probably only six or seven ever attended this "Colledge" and only one graduated from the University. We learn from Daniel Gookin, an expert on early Indian questions, of the difficulty of educating them, for some died after studying several years, while others were obliged to abandon their work when ready for college. A number of them returned to live with their tribes. This same authority makes the amusing remark that "Others were of the opinion, that Satan, the great enemy and opposer of men's salvation, who had for many years held these poor barbarians under his dominion, did use all his strategems and endeavours to impede the spreading of the Christian faith, that he might the better keep among them."

The only Indian actually to graduate from Harvard appears in the records with the rather longish name of Caleb Cheeshahteaumuck, "Indus"; it is spelled in the first Triennial Catalogue, printed in 1674, as Cheesechaumuck and later he was known as Cheeschaumuck. At the end of two Greek and Latin elegies he shortened his name still further to Cheesecaumuk, adding the words Senior Sophista. His Latin address to his benefactors is in the Royal Society of London. He was a son of a petty sachem of Holmes Hole (now Vineyard Haven) on Martha's Vineyard and was a member of the class of 1665, of which Governor Joseph Dudley, son of Governor Thomas Dudley, was also a member. The youngest son of Apostle John Eliot belonged to this same class, the total membership of which was only eight. Unfortunately the confinement indoors proved too much for Caleb's physique, and he died the following year, 1666, after taking his degree. Referring to the long Indian words, Cotton Mather used to say that they must have been growing ever since the confusion at Babel.

Another Indian from the same island was Joel Hiacoomes, who appears to have been a very promising lad. When still an undergraduate he was killed on a vacation just before commencement in 1665, at the hands of some Indians on Nantucket, where he was wrecked while returning to Boston with his father. Gookin said of him: "Thus perished our hopeful young prophet Joel. He was a good scholar and a pious man. . . . I knew him well, for he lived and was taught in the same town where I dwell." Joel wrote several sermons and gave lectures. Of these two scholars the same writer said: "These two were hopeful young men, especially Joel, being so ripe in learning, that he should within a few months have taken his first degree of bachelor of art in the College." Of Caleb he wrote: "The other called Caleb, not long after he took his degree of bachelor of art at Cambridge in New-England, died of a consumption at Charlestown, where he was placed by Mr. Thomas Danforth, who had inspection over him, under the care of a physician in order to his health; where he wanted not for the best means the country could afford, both of food and physick; but God denied the blessing, and put a period to his days." Danforth was a Boston member of the War Council and friend of Gookin.

President Chauncy said that both Caleb and Joel were called forth upon trial, at the Public Commencement, before the Magistrates and Elders, and in the face of the Country, and there upon very little warning gave great contentment to them that were present, they being examined in turning a part of a chapter in Isaiah into Latin, and showing the construction of it.

Gookin evidently remembered only these two Indians at Harvard. Another aborigine to attend the College was John Wampas, "Indian and Seaman," a petty chief from Grafton. Morison in his chapter on the Indian College makes the remark that if he did attend Harvard, he was wise enough to leave early instead of remaining to die. He is supposed to have learned some English while in Cambridge, but he could not have accumulated much learning, for he was obliged to make his mark to a document, presumably after leaving the school. He moved to Boston and took title to part of the land upon which Saint Paul's Cathedral in Boston now stands. Here he lived a curious existence among white people when not at sea or in jail in Boston or London. He was evidently a very disorderly citizen, for someone testified in 1677 that "since he came out of England, about 4 months past, he takes to no employment, but travils up and downe, in a vagrant, idle way." He died on another visit to England several years later.

The class of 1679 had an Indian called Eleazar who composed a Greek and Latin poem on the death of Reverend Thomas Thacher and did quite well, but did not graduate. He was the last to attend the Indian College.

One authority who purports to be a "Merchant of Boston" who communicated to his friend in London, in 1675 in a work entitled "The Present State of New England with respect to the Indian War," makes this statement in regard to an Indian student who attended Harvard before the erection of this Indian building: "About five or six Years since, there was brought up (amongst others) at the Colledg at Cambridg an Indian, named Sosomon, usually known as John Sassamon, of whom much has been written." He was born at Ponkapoag, became a convert to Christianity, helped the English in the Pequot war, learned our language and assisted Eliot in translating parts of the Bible into Indian. There is an entry on the Steward's records showing that he was at Harvard in 1653, therefore the London pamphlet, previously mentioned, was in error as to the date. He then became a teacher at Natick about 1660 and a short time later deserted to become King Philip's private secretary. He returned again to the English and was taken into one of their churches. He tried to convert this leader of the Wampanoags, gaining his enmity for so doing. He was ordered to prison and on the way there was murdered. Those who committed the crime were caught by the English. Philip became so éxasperated that he wanted his revenge and this led to the great Indian War. Sassamon's life was an eventful and romantic one, and he often has been called the first Christian Indian martyr.

Many years later, in 1716, appears the name of another Indian, Benjamin Larnel, probably the last of his race to attend Harvard. On May 9, 1713 the records show a sum of 16 pounds 17/6 paid Andrew Bordman, the College Steward, according to a vote of the Corporation, for "ye use and maintenance of Larnel, an Indian, ½ a year from ye time of his admission wch ws 5th 9ber, 1712." He was dismissed for some misconduct during his Junior year, but was restored to good standing by a public confession, which President Leverett mentions as of "a peculiar grace," which "ratified wonderfully that which I had conceived of him." He, too, died soon afterwards, before finishing his course, and is described by the President as "an Acute Grammarian, an Extraordinary Latin Poet, and a good Greek one."

John and Thomas Stanton, sons of a well-known interpreter employed by the English, also went to Harvard at an early date. The former evidently did not behave any too well, because he was reprimanded for "slinging stones at Mr. Stedman's glass Windowes."

There are several official votes relating to the students at the Indian College that may be of interest. The Plymouth Colony records for September, 1659, in reply to the Corporation in England, state that "There are fiue Indian youthes att Cambridge in the lattin Scoole; whose dilligence and profisiency in theire studdies doth much encurrage vs to hope that god is fiting them and preparing them for good Instruments in this great and desirable works wee haue good Testimony from those that are prudent and pious that they are dilligent in theire studdies and ciuell in theire carriage; and from the Presedent of the Colledge, seruants the Comissioners of the vnited Collonies, Hartford the 7th of Septem: 1659 JOHN WINTHORPE, Presedent." There is another reference to this same subject in the Records of the Governor and Company of Massachusetts Bay in the year 1665, the vote of the Court reading: "Concerning the civillizing and instructing the Indians in the knowledge of God and humajne learning, there is a smale colledge or fabricke of bricke erected in Cambridge, particularly appropriated to the Indians, which was built on the accompt and by the order of the corporation; there are eight Indian youths, one whereof is in the colledge, and ready to comence batchiler of art, besides another, in the like capacity, a few months since, wth seuerall English, was murdered by the Indians at Nantucket; and at other schools some ready to come into the collidge" etc. An-

OLD INDIAN CHURCH (Mashpee)
This Indian church on Cape Cod is supported largely from funds received from the Williams' bequest through Harvard University.

other reference to this establishment was made by Hugh Peters, teacher of the First Church in Salem, who in a letter to a minister in Virginia remarked that "Wee have a printery here, and thinke to goe to worke with some speciall things, and if you have any thing you may sent it safely."

Among the books in the Harvard College Library are several sent to the University by the well-known Joseph Brant, who made the translations himself. They were acknowledged by Joseph Willard, the President, under vote of the President and Fellows, June 5, 1789, reading as follows: "That the thanks of this Corporation be presented to Colonel Joseph Brant, Chief of the Mohawk Nation, for his polite attention to this University, in his kind donation to its Library of the Book of Common Prayer of the Church of England, with the Gospel of Mark, translated into the Mohawk language, and a Primer in the same language." The former volume seems to be the only one to be found there today. The reception of this distinguished Mohawk in the British Capital is told in our first Indian booklet.

Harvard University is still helping the Indians of Massachusetts under the will of Reverend Daniel Williams of London. This fund dates from 1716 and was provided "to manage the Blessed Work of Converting the poor Indians there." From the income the Treasurer of the College furnishes a certain amount towards the salary of the Minister of the Indian Church at Mashpee on Cape Cod and another sum is donated to the Society for Propagating the Gospel among the Indians and Others in North America. This latter Society was established in 1787 and has been active ever since, employing the services of an excellent travelling missionary, Gustave E. E. Lindquist. Another bequest was made by Robert Boyle, F.R.S., the well-known English chemist who was governor of the Society with the long name. He was interested in educating and converting the Indians of New England, and was besides a staunch supporter of the work of John Eliot. He supplied funds for the second edition of the Bible. In his will Boyle left a fund of £400 "to be set aside and employed as a stock for the relief of poor Indian converts." Of this fund the executor decided to give £55 annually to Harvard for the payment of the ministers to preach to the natives; a similar sum to the Society that supported John Eliot, and the remainder for Indian education at William and Mary College in Virginia. The first Boyle payment provided a scholarship for Benjamin Larnel, and the next went to pay for his funeral. The churches of Boston in the year 1718 contributed £483 toward converting the Indians.

Without going into too many details we believe we should mention the different printing presses that were in use at Harvard, at least one of them having been located in the Indian building. Cambridge became the home of the first hand printing press in the English Colonies of America when in

Kindness of the late P. H. Lombard

BRONZE TABLET ON STONE IN FRONT OF INDIAN CHURCH ESTABLISHED AT MASHPEE BY RICHARD BOURNE. DEDICATED SEPTEMBER 9, 1923 by PRESIDENT LOWELL

1638 Stephen Daye, of London, and three pressmen arrived in Boston with one. It was known as the Cambridge press and was set up in the house of the President of the University, Henry Dunster. It was probably never set up in the Indian Building. It was managed by Daye until 1649, when it was taken over by Samuel Green. The Vermont Historical Society of Montpelier now possesses this "Daye Press," as it is called, the most interesting relic connected with American typography. At the time of the graduation of Harvard's first class, in 1642, a tract entitled "New England's First Fruits" appeared off this press. The first part gives an account of the earliest attempts to civilize and convert the Indians of Massachusetts. Three years later, in 1645, "A Declaration of Former Passages and Proceedings Betwixt the English and the Narrowgansets" issued from the first press by order of the Commissioners for the United Colonies. It was printed in English by Daye and signed by "Jo: Winthrop, President, for the Commissioners." Several copies are in existence. Another book to come off this early press was the Indian Primer or "Cattichisme of the Indian langwige," printed by Samuel Green, the College printer, in 1654, and written by John Eliot, which was the earliest printed Indian book in the "Massachusetts Indian Language," as Eliot usually called it, of which we have any record. Other works to appear were the Book of Genesis and the Gospel of Matthew, both translated into the Indian language by the same author, who began the study of the Indian language as early as 1643. There are no examples of the earlier editions of these Indian works known to be in existence.

The second printing press was sent to Cambridge in the autumn of 1659 by the Corporation for the Propagation of the Gospel among the Indians in New England in order to facilitate the publication of Eliot's Indian Bible, which was now ready to be set up. This Corporation at first had its printing executed in London, but as the Indians began to read at Cambridge and elsewhere, it was thought best that the treatises should be printed in America where those who made the translations could more carefully follow the work. This second press was installed probably soon after its arrival in the Indian building, which according to experts was well suited to that business, and as authority for this statement we mention Daniel Gookin, who was appointed in 1662 one of the first two licensers of the press.

About this time Eliot needed help and wrote abroad for an assistant, suggesting that he "serve you here in New-England at the presse in Harvard Colledge, and work under the Colledge Printer, in impressing the Bible in the Indian language." Accordingly Marmaduke Johnson was dispatched to this country in 1660. Johnson was a skilled typographer and was of great value to Green in helping him print the Indian Bible. The translation required many years' study on the part of Rev. John Eliot, "Apostle to the Indians," particularly as the Indian vocabulary was so very limited. It was a labor of love and was one of the most extraordinary examples of skill and perseverance ever shown. Eliot at one time served as a member of the Board of Overseers of the College. The actual printing of the New Testament in the Mohegan Indian dialect, the language of all New England Indians, was begun in the late autumn of 1659 under the supervision of Samuel Green, the College Printer, with the aid of his Indian pupil, "James." They experienced great difficulty in setting up the type of an entirely new language, different from any other. Eliot, in speaking of his difficulty in attaining proficiency, wrote that the language had its latitudes and corners. Part of it was undoubtedly printed on this second press installed in the Indian "Colledge" or building. It is interesting to remember that some of the type was furnished by Hezekiah Usher, a well-known merchant of Boston, who also supplied much of the paper. Ratcliffe, who bound the books, complained of the high cost of living in Boston at that time. The work went ahead at the rate of eight pages a week. After about a year of almost steady work the New Testament was finished, in 1661, and two years later, in the autumn of 1663, the complete Bible of 1200 pages was printed, this edition consisting of several thousand copies, the greatest achievement of the Cambridge Presses and the first Bible to be printed in the New World. Samuel E. Morison, in his History of Harvard University, gives this version of the work that was then being performed: "Almost any day the students, when passing through the yard, could peer through the windows of the Indian College, and watch the Indian 'devil,' James Printer, sweating at the hand lever, Marmaduke feeding in sheets of paper and removing them with that neat-fingered deftness of the trained printer, and Sergeant Green setting up type for the next sheet."

Cotton Mather, who said that the Indian words were of "sesquipedalian and unaccountable dimensions," refers to this work in this way: "This Bible was printed in all America, from the very foundation of the world" ". . . The whole translation was writ with but one pen, which pen, had it not been lost, would have certainly deserved a richer case than was bestowed upon that pen with which Holland writ his translation of Plutarch." Holland, after making one of his well-known translations, composed this verse:

"With one sole pen I writ this book,
Made of a gray goose quill;
A pen it was, when I it took
And a pen I leave it still."

74

Another student of this same subject, Isaiah Thomas, declared that "It was a work of so much consequence as to arrest the attention of the nobility and gentry of England, as well as that of King Charles, to whom it was dedicated. The Press of Harvard College, in Cambridge, Massachusetts, was for a time, as celebrated as the presses of the universities of Oxford and Cambridge, in England." As soon as the complete Bible was finished, a copy of each testament was forwarded to the King and forty other copies were sent to England. The full title of the whole work

MAMUSSE
WUNNEETUPANATAMWE
UP-BIBLUM GOD
NANEESWE
NUKKONE TESTAMENT
KAH WONK
WUSKU TESTAMENT.

Ne quoshkinnumuk nashpe Wuttinneumoh *CHRIST*
noh asoowesit

JOHN ELIOT

CAMBRIDGE:
Printeuoop nashpe *Samuel Green* kah *Marmaduke Johnson*.
1 6 6 3.

From "Bibliographic Notes on Eliot's Indian Bible and on his Other Translations and Works in the Indian Language of Massachusetts"
FACSIMILE OF THE INDIAN TITLE-PAGE OF THE WHOLE BIBLE OF 1663
This colossal work of translating the Bible into the Indian tongue was performed in an amazingly short time by John Eliot.

was "Mamusse Wunneetupanatamwe Up-Biblum God, Naneeswe Nukkone Testament kah wonk Wusku Testament", etc. Naturally there were some mistakes in making the translation. One of the most amusing was the misuse of the word "eel-pot" for "lattice," making the sentence read "The mother of Sisera looked out at a window, and cried through the eel-pot." Copies of this first 1663 edition of the entire Bible are extremely rare. The copy in Jesus College of Cambridge, England, where the translator received his degree in 1622, was forwarded to the college by Eliot himself with this notation, a translation of which is: "To Jesus College — Accept, mother, I pray, what a most humble alumnus offers, a son ever having thy prayers."

The second edition, which came out in 1685, was revised by John Cotton of Plymouth, who also had made a study of the Indian dialect.

From 1655 to 1672 one hundred books were issued from the two presses at Cambridge, and of this number fifteen were in the Indian dialect. One curious and amusing title of the last Indian book bearing the Cambridge imprint was "Spiritual Milk for Babes in either England, drawn out of the Breasts of both Testaments for the Nourishment of their Souls." At a later date appeared in Boston a tract with the odd title: "The Hatchets, to hew down the Tree of Sin, which bears the Fruit of Death." The best seller of that day, however, was the "Day of Doom" written by Michael Wigglesworth in 1662. Samuel A. Drake refers to the situation at the press in these words: "History does not tell how many eyes were spoiled, and how many jaws were broken, in Cambridge, in the course of printing John Eliot's Indian Bible; but doubtless Mr. Samuel Green and Mr. Marmaduke Johnson could have furnished materials for a record."

Several well-known Indians lent a helping hand in the Harvard printing establishment. One of these assistants was a Nipmuck known as James, to which name "Printer" was added after he had shown his ability in this line of work. He often went by the nickname of "Wowaus." He received instruction at the Indian charity school, at Cambridge, and then became an apprentice to Samuel Green. He served in the press office for sixteen years and then suddenly decided in 1675 to give up work, return to live and take sides with his compatriots. A year later he availed himself of the opportunity to come back to the English ranks and receive immunity. He returned to the printing business in Cambridge and resumed his work there, giving most of his time to getting out the second edition of the Bible to take the place of the former books, most of which were burned or lost in King Philip's War. He is named with B. Green as one of the printers of the Psalter that appeared in 1709. The successful printing of the Bible is due in large measure to James Printer, of whom Eliot wrote in 1683 to his friend Robert Boyle in London, ". . . we have but one man, viz. the Indian Printer, that is able to compose the sheets, and correct the press with understanding." Weetamoe, about whom we had a chapter in our first Indian booklet, mentions that James acted as go-between to effect her release. Some of his descendants lived for some time afterwards at the Indian settlement in Grafton. The other Indian to assist Eliot was named Job Nesutan, a Mohegan living on Long Island. The "Apostle," realizing he could make little progress in converting the Indians through his own language, resolved to learn their dialect which, of course, was a most difficult task. He first received instructions from Cockenoe, of Long Island — known also as Cheekanob, who had been captured in the Pequot War; later he engaged Nesutan, an old Indian, to live in his family and to teach him. It has been claimed that Eliot acquired the new tongue in a few months, and made use of it for the first time at the Christian Indian settlement at Nonantum, now Newton. According to Gookin, Nesutan was "A very good linguist in the English tongue, and was Mr. Eliot's assistant and interpreter in his translation of the Bible and other books in the Indian language." He proved himself to be a daring soldier when with the English on the first expedition to Mt. Hope, Rhode Island.

Morison sums up the Indian College in this manner: "Even now one reflects with sorrow on poor Joel, Caleb and Eleazer, imbued with ambition to be the schoolmasters and saviors of their people, toiling against every healthy instinct of their race to achieve that proficiency in the Seven Arts and Learned Tongues without which, so their white masters insisted, they could never qualify as purveyors of regenerating grace."

HANNAH DUSTIN STATUE IN G. A. R. PARK, HAVERHILL, MASSACHUSETTS
Dedicated to her bravery. The four scenes connected with her history at this time
are depicted on the monument. It is in a conspicuous place, but few of the many passers-by
realize that it stands there as a permanent memorial to this heroine of Haverhill.

HANNAH DUSTIN OF HAVERHILL

Hannah Dustin shares with Whittier the distinction of being Haver-hill's foremost citizen. In fact, the people of that place, called at that time Pentucket, have paid signal honor to this brave woman by placing in G. A. R. Park, now known as Grand Army Park, a monu-ment to her heroism. The many motorists on their way to Amesbury or taking the other fork of the road leading to Manchester, New Hampshire, pass close to the figure of Hannah Dustin on a high pedestal, with a tomahawk in her right hand, without realizing at all the meaning of this memorial and without appreciating this unique and daring episode in the life of a resident of that city. Cotton Mather, who interviewed her in Boston after her escape from cap-tivity, refers to the incident as a "notable exploit," in describing the story of her capture and release in his *"Magnalia Christi Americana,"* published in England in 1702. The family name is also often spelled Duston or Dustan, the wording differing even on the two memorials in her town. Concerning this surname, some wit made the sugges-tion that the original member of the family to remove to this country must undoubtedly have been a descendant of the St. Dunstan in the legends who vanquished the Devil by pinching his nose with a pair of red-hot tongs. Those who have studied the history of the family state that the Thomas Dustin of Haverhill descended from the Dun-stans of England.

Haverhill, which was at the time merely a small frontier settlement, was invaded by a band of Indians on March 15, 1697, and the Dustin house was the first one to be attacked. Hannah Dustin's husband, Thomas, who was a former constable of the town, was either chopping wood or working at his brick kiln, situated probably near the present Hilldale Street, fragments of which could be seen until quite recently.

77

Kindness of Albert G. Harding
Haverhill Historical Society

TOMAHAWK USED BY HANNAH DUSTIN TO DISPATCH SEVERAL OF HER TEN CAPTORS

The scalping knife she used, and other articles, are valued possessions of the Haverhill Historical Society.

He undoubtedly heard the war-whoops of the approaching redskins and, mounting his horse, made haste home in hope of being able to place his family in safety in the garrison house. He reached his dwelling in time to order his seven children to flee for their lives, and then hurried to the bedside of his wife, who a week before had given birth to an eighth child, a daughter named Martha. Four other children had died previous to this time. The attacking party was seen approaching, and the unfortunate father was now obliged to decide whether it would be best to try to save any of his seven children, or to stay with his wife and endeavor to rescue her. Before she could rise from her bed, however, the Indians were upon them and, as there seemed to be no hope of preserving her and the infant, he reluctantly mounted his horse and dashed after his fleeing family. It was his intention to save only one of his children, but they all looked at him so appealingly that he decided to defend them in the hope of beating off the enemy and saving the lives of all. He therefore dismounted, and placing himself in the rear of his seven offspring, kept the attacking Indians at bay by dexterous use of his gun. For a mile or so the battle raged, until finally they retreated to a garrison house on Pecker's Hill which served them as a temporary refuge. At this point the redskins gave up the fight, as they evidently preferred to take part in the pillaging of the settlement. Fortunately none of the Dustin family was hit.

Many of the inhabitants fled to this same garrison house, on Pecker's Hill near by, a more recent building later used for the same purpose being today still in existence. Concerning this former fortress, there is handed down to us an amusing story which took place a month later. One of the occupants at the time of the massacre was a bachelor who, after refraining from matrimony for many years, finally fell in love with a woman who continually spurned his affections. He became very desperate and informed her that he intended to throw himself down the well which was situated near by. Upon reaching the spot, so the story goes, he decided it would not be worth while to fling away his life on such a hard-hearted creature. By chance he happened to notice a large log close by, and he at once conceived the idea of hurling it into the well instead of himself. He then hid behind a tree to await results. The object of his attentions, upon hearing the splash, completely relented and felt sorry she had rejected her suitor. She thereupon rushed to the well and shouted

From "History of Middlesex County, Massachusetts," Volume II, by Samuel Adams Drake
Published Boston, 1880, by Estes & Lauriat

ESCAPE OF THOMAS DUSTIN OF HAVERHILL, MASSACHUSETTS, AND
SEVEN OF HIS CHILDREN

At the time of the massacre of that town on March 15, 1697. His wife was captured in their house, and their recently born baby was killed. The wife, nurse and a boy called Leonardson made a miraculous escape from Contoocook, just north of Concord, New Hampshire. She is the heroine of Haverhill.

out, "Joseph, Joseph, if you are in the land of the living, I will have you." Joseph, with a smile of amusement on his face, appeared from his hiding place, and they became engaged at once.

To return to the ill and distracted wife, we learn that with her was a friend and neighbor, called Mrs. Mary Corliss Neff, who at that time was nursing her. The latter tried to escape with the infant, but was caught as she was leaving the house. After proceeding a short distance the child began to cry, whereupon the pursuers dashed out her brains on an apple tree near by. Haverhillites for many years afterwards used to relate that they had eaten apples from this same tree which marked the tragedy. The Indians then commanded Hannah Dustin to rise and dress, and while she was collecting a few clothes she watched the intruders rifle and then set fire to the building. Thinly clad, especially for a March day, the mother with only one shoe, the women were led by their captors in a northerly direction about twelve miles. For a number of days they marched through snow and mud until they arrived at an island called Contoocook, which is situated at the junction of the Merrimack and Contoocook Rivers in the town of Penacook, about six miles north of Concord, New Hampshire. This attractive wooded island contains about two acres of land, and the river served as a strong fortification against attack. It is also now known by the name of Dustin Island. Today the Northern Railroad, a part of the Boston and Maine system, crosses the island. The distance from Haverhill is about sixty miles, but the travellers, it is believed, traversed about one hundred and fifty miles, as they went

Kindness of Clarence S. Brigham, Director,
American Antiquarian Society, Worcester

TABLET ON THE SITE OF THE
HOME OF SAMUEL LENORSON
(OR LEONARDSON) IN WORCESTER
The inscription reads:
"On this site stood the home of Samuel
Lenorson. This tablet is erected in memory
of his son Samuel who at twelve years of age
was stolen by the Indians in 1695. His master
joined in the attack on Haverhill in 1697,
assisting in the capture of Mrs. Dustin and
Mrs. Neff.
"On the march toward Canada while encamped on an island near Concord, N. H.,
these captives, led by Mrs. Dustin, killed ten
of the Indians and thus regaining their liberty
returned to their homes."
Another tablet has been placed on the front
of Davis Tower, in Lake Park near Lake
Quinsigamond, where Leonardson was kid-
napped.

by very circuitous paths to avoid capture. One of the Indians lived at this delightful spot, his family consisting of two men, three women and seven children, and an English boy fourteen years of age, called Samuel Leonardson, who had been captured at Worcester in a raid about eighteen months before.

Contoocook was about halfway to their destination, which was in Canada; it was now the night of March 29th–30th. The captives had just been informed that when they reached the next settlement they would have to run the gauntlet, which was a disagreeable and even dangerous Indian custom usually imposed upon their white prisoners. Hannah Dustin and her friend preferred to risk their lives now and, in an effort to escape, imitate the action of "Jael and Sisera," as one writer expressed it.

Hannah urged Leonardson to endeavor to find out from one of their captors where to strike a person in order to kill him instantly, and also how to scalp him. The unsuspecting warrior laid his finger on his temple, and said in very broken English, "Strike 'em there." This information was promptly conveyed to Mrs. Dustin, who determined to make a bid for freedom that same night. The Indians had turned in to rest and, as Herbert M. Sylvester describes it: "The smoke of the camp fire trails off toward the river, as if beckoning her to freedom. She hears the surge of the river, for the March rains have swollen it to freshet-pitch, to fill the woods with its dull roar. It is sweet music. For her, the dark of this night is full of welcome." She aroused her friend and the English boy and gave the signal. The tomahawks rain on their victims like lightning as the three glide among the twelve sleeping Indians. Hannah Dustin tomahawked her master, while Leonardson dispatched the same redskin who told him where to hit a death blow. The Indian who killed her child was also one of the victims. Only two escaped, an old woman badly mutilated, and an Indian boy whom the avengers desired to preserve, and these two took to the woods in great fear. The three daring people who had performed this unparalleled deed now hasten to the borders of the Merrimack and, using great foresight, scuttle all the

From "A Popular History of the United States," Vol. III, by William Cullen Bryant and Sydney Howard Gay. New York: Kindness of Charles Scribner's Sons

HANNAH DUSTIN'S WONDERFUL ESCAPE FROM CONTOOCOOK ISLAND IN NEW HAMPSHIRE

canoes with the exception of the one they intend to use in their descent of the river which is to lead them back to Haverhill. With the guns, tomahawks and knives of the dead Indians and some food, they start off in their craft, but before proceeding very far Hannah Dustin realizes that her unusual story will probably never be believed by her friends unless she can produce the scalps themselves. So they paddle back to the island and pack their ten gory relics in a linen cloth which she had probably taken with her on her trip north. A piece of this cloth and other Dustin trophies are objects of great interest in the Dustin showcase of the Haverhill Historical Society, housed in "The Buttonwoods," an attractive old building which stands on the site of one of the Saltonstall homes.

Their flight down the river was more perilous than one would naturally suppose, owing to the many bands of Indians lurking along the banks, but fortunately they reached their destination safely. One of the three always stayed awake during the journey. Hannah Dustin presented herself before her astonished husband who never again expected to see her, and she was equally surprised and pleased to find him and their seven children alive and well. They are supposed to have landed in a part of the city known as Willowdale at Bradley's Brook, which is on the river road to Lawrence. There is a public landing there now, and a millstone shown in a cut has been placed there to commemorate this event. There is a similar marker, at Dustin Dam, and another memorial on the old Indian trail near Concord Street, almost opposite the lake which was renamed by Whittier "Kenoza," the aboriginal word for "pickerel." Several places lower down the river claim to have housed the three fugitives on their first

*Kindness of Albert G. Harding,
Haverhill Historical Society*

MARKER AT BRADLEY'S LANDING ON BRADLEY'S BROOK IN THE WIL-LOWDALE DISTRICT, HAVERHILL, WHERE HANNAH DUSTIN LANDED ON HER RETURN DOWN THE RIVER FROM CONTOOCOOK ISLAND
It is situated near the highway on the road running from Lawrence to Haverhill, and near the Methuen line. There is a similar marker on an Indian trail near the Concord Road at Kenoza Lake, near by.

stopping place, and two markers in two different places actually claim that they spent the night there. Some authorities believe that they first stopped at Nathan Tyng's house in Tyngsboro, and it seems to be definite that on the same evening they moved to and spent the night at the dwelling of Captain John Lovewell at Dunstable, now part of Nashua. Pictures of the Lovewell marker appear here. It is supposed that they spent the last night before reaching Haverhill at the Bradley homestead, which is located at a place where Creek Brook flows into the Merrimack.

After having recuperated from her trying experiences of the past days, the heroine of Haverhill and her husband, with Mary Neff and the boy, journeyed to Boston on April 21st to relate her story. It is said that they had with them the gun belonging to an Indian she slew, also the tomahawk and knife which they had used in their gruesome task, and likewise the ten scalps to serve as evidence of their deed, all of which impressed so greatly the General Court of Massachusetts that on June 8th Hannah Dustin was awarded "out of the publick treasury" twenty-five pounds, and to her companions twelve pounds ten shillings each, to give them all a fresh start in life. It has also been stated that a number of persons gave her presents of different kinds. It was at this time that Rev. Cotton Mather talked to her and wrote the first story of this event as already mentioned. The story of their escape spread afar, and Governor Nicholson of Maryland as a mark of his regard sent her a present of a pewter tankard, which is now owned by Henry Merrill of Exeter, N.H. A picture of it appears in the text, as well as an illustration showing the tomahawk. Some years later, in 1739, Joseph,

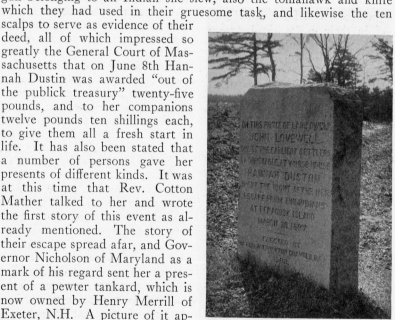

*Kindness of Albert G. Harding
Haverhill Historical Society*

TABLET TO HANNAH DUSTIN ON THE PLACE OF CAPTAIN JOHN LOVEWELL, SHOWING THE INSCRIPTION son of Mary Neff, petitioned "The Great and General Court" for a grant of land in consideration of his mother's captivity, and of her services in assisting Hannah Dustin "in killing divers Indians," alleging "on their return home, they passed through the utmost hazard of their lives, and suffered distressing want, being almost starved before they could return to their dwellings."

In order to get a more vivid idea of this exploit and the Dustin surroundings, a visit to Haverhill is very necessary. The writer was fortunate in being shown these localities and objects of interest by Albert L. Harding, whose wife is a descendant of Hannah Dustin.

The house in which they lived when attacked was probably situated on the corner of Hilldale and Endora Streets. Permission was refused to place a memorial of some kind here, therefore one was placed on the plot of land on Monument Street, which leads off Hilldale Street, where her son Jonathan resided and where Hannah died. Here stands a huge boulder, shown in an illustration, which was drawn into position by sixteen horses. On the front of the monument appears "Hannah Dustan, March 30, 1697" and beneath is the name of her husband. Dustin Street and Dustin School are near by, and instead of war-whoops and yells one hears the laughter and shouts of the children at play. Two bull's-eye lights from the garrison house are now in the Historical Society and are all that are left.

There is an interesting story connected with an earlier memorial which was placed in 1861 on the property where they lived at the time of the massacre. On the front were carved the implements of that day, bow and arrow, musket, scalping knife and tomahawk, while on the other sides appeared the names of Dustin's ancestors and those of an Emerson. Her

Kindness of Albert G. Harding, Haverhill Historical Society

MARKER ON CAPTAIN JOHN LOVEWELL'S PLACE AT DUNSTABLE, NOW PART OF NASHUA, NEW HAMPSHIRE
Here Hannah Dustin and her two companions spent the first night after their deliverance, March 30, 1697. A photograph of the tablet itself appears elsewhere.

Kindness of Albert G. Harding Haverhill Historical Society

PEWTER TANKARD PRESENTED TO HANNAH DUSTIN BY GOVERNOR FRANCIS NICHOLSON OF MARYLAND
This interesting relic is now owned by Harry Merrill of Exeter, N.H.

Kindness of Albert G. Harding

BOULDER IN TRANSIT TO ITS REST-
ING PLACE ON MONUMENT STREET,
WHERE HANNAH DUSTIN WAS LIV-
ING WITH HER SON JONATHAN AT
THE TIME OF HER DEATH

killing of the enemy and the de-
fense of their children by the
father were shown on the two
other tablets. The war interfered
with the subscriptions and litiga-
tion ensued, resulting in the unusual ceremony of removing the
monument four years later to the
public square at Barre, Massachusetts, where it now serves as
a soldiers' memorial, the tablets of
course having been removed. Few
people who pass through that
town are aware of the amusing
history of this marker, which was
first made and set up in honor of
a Haverhill woman.

There is still another Dustin dwelling, shown in an illustration, which
was built by a younger generation of the family and which stood near
Dustin Square on North Main Street, which road leads toward
Plaistow, New Hampshire. With these names attached to many
places connected with the life of Hannah Dustin, it would seem as if
she had been notably honored, especially when one considers the large
memorial placed in Haverhill's G. A. R. Park in 1879. This latter monument is exceedingly impressive and the four bronze reliefs, one on each
side, are very well done. They depict her capture, the husband's de-
fense, her slaying of her captors, and the return down the Merrimack.
The name appears here as Duston. Not long ago Hannah seemed still
to have an enemy in her home town insulting her memory (as someone humorously expressed it) when a driverless automobile ran on a
mad career down Main Street. On reaching Hotel Bartlett it swerved
directly toward the monument, but fortunately when close to the sur-
rounding iron railing, turned off again in time to avoid hitting it.
Some rascal stole the hatchet from the statue, but it has been replaced.

On Contoocook
Island, the scene
of her escape, the
citizens of N e w
Hampshire have
s e t u p another
monument which
shows her on a
high p e d e s t a l,
tomahawk in one
hand and several
scalps in the other.
This curious in-
scription may also
be seen: "The
W a r - W h o o p
Tomahawk Fag-
got and Infanti-

Published by W. H. Wood,
Haverhill, Mass.

HANNAH DUSTIN MEMORIAL, HAVERHILL
After being placed in position on Monument Street, where
Hannah Dustin died. The place of the massacre is unmarked.
Dustin Street and Dustin School are near by.

cides were at Haverhill. The Ashes of Wigwam-Camp-Fires at Night and of Ten of the Tribe are Here." The Northern Railroad crosses the island at its widest part, about 700 feet, and the monument is about sixty feet east of the railroad track. The only access to the monument is by a walk on the side of the railroad bridge.

The eight children of Thomas and Hannah grew up, and their descendants are numerous, coming from far and wide to attend the annual gatherings at Haverhill. Hannah Dustin was one of fifteen children of Michael and Hannah (Webster) Emerson. She was

Kindness of Albert G. Harding
Haverhill Historical Society.

A DUSTIN RESIDENCE BUILT BY A YOUNGER GENERATION OF THE FAMILY SITUATED IN DUSTIN SQUARE, HAVERHILL

Kindness W. S. Trowbridge, Vice-President Boston & Maine Railroad, and the Superintendent of State Buildings in New Hampshire

MONUMENT TO HANNAH DUSTIN OF HAVERHILL, MASSACHUSETTS ON CONTOOCOOK OR DUSTIN ISLAND, AT THE JUNCTION OF THE MERRIMACK AND CONTOO-COOK RIVERS AT PENACOOK, NEW HAMPSHIRE. A LEASED LINE OF THE BOSTON AND MAINE RAILROAD PASSES NEARBY

Here on the night of March 29-30, 1697, this brave woman, with the help of her nurse, Mary Neff, and a Worcester lad, killed her Indian captives and made her way back to her native city. On the front appear the words in Latin for "Brave in Deed"—"Trusting in Justice". On the back appear the date and this inscription: "The War Whoop Tomahawk Faggot & Infanticides Were at Haverhill. The Ashes of Wigwam-Camp-Fires at Night & of Ten of the Tribe Are Here." (Her name is here spelled Duston.)

born on December 23, 1657, and married Thomas Dustin twenty years later. The husband and others of the family are buried in the Pentucket Cemetery, but the resting place of Hannah has never been discovered, doubtless due to the fact that she was probably buried in some secret place in order that the Indians could not retaliate and defile her grave. Dustin Mountain at Dartmouth College serves as a permanent memorial to the family.

Mary E. Desmond, in her article dealing with this event, says: "The story is a thrilling one, and it proves that women in all ages have risen to the occasion when bravery was needed, and none responded with more courage and strength of character than this heroine of the long ago, Hannah Dustin."

In 1863, a family of Dustins, while moving from Waverly, Minnesota, were ambushed by Indians and all killed but two, who were left for dead. The remains of the dead were buried near by, and in 1927 during excavation were discovered. In an account in the *St. Paul Dispatch* a neighbor, who was asked to accompany them at the time of the massacre, said that the Indians had an old grudge against a member of a Dustin family, and that, in the belief of the red men, was sufficient to condemn all Dustins to the same sort of vengeance.

From an old print formerly owned by the State Street Trust Co., but now in the collection of a resident of Anawan Road in Waban

ANNAWON ROCK, WHERE THE INDIAN CHIEF OF THIS NAME, ONE OF KING PHILIP'S LEADING WARRIORS, WAS CAPTURED BY BENJAMIN CHURCH, SHORTLY AFTER THE GREAT SWAMP FIGHT AT SOUTH KINGSTON, RHODE ISLAND

Its location is in the southeastern part of Rehoboth, about eight miles from Taunton, on the southeasterly side of the road leading from Taunton to Providence. It is a large rock and quite near the road. The children of the neighborhood play "big Injun" games around it.

Kindness of John W. Haley

"NINE MEN'S MISERY" TABLET AT "CAMP SWAMP" IN TOWN OF CUMBERLAND, RHODE ISLAND

The scene of the slaughter and burial place of nine of a colonial contingent, under Captain Michael Pierce. These nine men survived the earlier fight against a band of Indians under Canonchet, which took place in 1676 at Central Falls several miles away, near Pawtucket, Rhode Island. The location of this memorial is in a secluded spot on the grounds of the Cistercian Monastery which is situated on the Diamond Hill road between Wrentham and Pawtucket.

Kindness of John W. Haley

TABLET AT CENTRAL FALLS, NEAR PAWTUCKET, RHODE ISLAND

Marking the spot where "Captain Michael Pierce and his company of Plymouth Colonists, ambushed and outnumbered, were almost annihilated by the Indians, March 26, 1676." It is placed at the upper part of High Street, a little north of the archway under the Providence and Boston Railroad bridge.

From a print   *Kindness of Chester H. Phillips*

ROGER WILLIAMS MEETING INDIANS AT "WHAT CHEER" ROCK ON
WEST SHORE OF SEEKONK RIVER, 1636

Kindness of John W. Haley

"WHAT CHEER" ROCK MONUMENT
AT CORNER OF POWER AND GANO
STREETS, PROVIDENCE, RHODE
ISLAND

Erected to commemorate the place where
Roger Williams and the Indians first met.
The words on one side are "And having of
a sense of God's merciful Providence unto
me in my distress called the place Providence. I desired it might be for a shelter
for persons distressed for conscience."—
Roger Williams.

Kindness of John W. Haley

ANOTHER VIEW OF "WHAT CHEER" ROCK AS IT APPEARED AROUND THE
MIDDLE OF THE LAST CENTURY

Photographed by Milton M. Cranston   *Kindness of John W. Haley and Milton M. Cranston*
LOCATION OF POMHAM'S FORT NOT FAR FROM ROCKY POINT ON WARWICK
NECK, ON THE EASTERLY SHORE OF OLD WARWICK COVE, WARWICK,
RHODE ISLAND
This fort was built in 1644 for this Indian Sachem, Pomham, by his "English Allies as
a defence against the 'bluddymindedness' of the Narragansetts," to quote from a tablet
placed on this promontory. The remnants of this structure are supposed to be "earliest
handiwork of man now extant in Rhode Island," to quote the words of the late Howard M.
Chapin of the Rhode Island Historical Society. Pomham fought against the colonists in
King Philip's War and was killed in a fight in Dedham Woods, in Massachusetts.

*From Metacom's Grand March. Composed for and respectfully dedicated to his friend John W.
Dearth, Esq., of Bristol, R.I., by Oliver J. Shaw*
WESTERN VIEW OF MOUNT HOPE
The residence of the renowned Indian warrior King Philip, with a distant view of Fall
River and the Bay. This attractive property is owned by R. F. Haffenreffer.

From "Yamoyden," by Rev. James Wallis Eastburn, A.M., and Robert C. Sands

SEAT OF KING PHILIP, AT MOUNT HOPE, BRISTOL, RHODE ISLAND, THE ESTATE OF R. F. HAFFENREFFER.

Kindness of John W. Haley

MASSASOIT SPRING AND TABLET AT SOWAMS, NOW PART OF WARREN, RHODE ISLAND

Near here was the favorite seat of Massasoit, great leader of the Wampanoags. The Pilgrims made two journeys to Sowams, one in 1621 and the other two years later. Edward Winslow, Stephen Hopkins and the faithful Squanto went on the first journey; Winslow, John Hampden and Hobomok made the second journey.

Kindness of John W. Haley

KING PHILIP MONUMENT, AT MOUNT HOPE, BRISTOL, RHODE ISLAND

Near the spot where this chieftain was killed by an Indian ally called John Aldeman, on August 12, O. S. 1676. It is located in the woods on the Mount Hope estate of R. F. Haffenreffer.

Kindness of R. F. Haffenreffer

RARE DUGOUT CANOE IN THE MUSEUM OF R. F. HAFFENREFFER AT MOUNT HOPE, BRISTOL, RHODE ISLAND

From a print in the Indian Collection of R. F. Haffenreffer at Mount Hope, Bristol, R.I.

ACTUAL COPPER NECKLACE AND REPLICA OF THE PIPE FROM MASSA-SOIT'S GRAVE IN THE INDIAN BUR-IAL GROUND AT BURR'S HILL, WAR-REN, RHODE ISLAND

This is supposed to be the necklace given to Massasoit by the Pilgrims to be used as identification by any of the messengers sent by this Chieftain to the Plymouth Colony. The original pipe is in the Heye Museum of New York City.

Kindness of John W. Haley

SITE OF ORIGINAL HOME OF BEN-JAMIN CHURCH, IN LITTLE COMP-TON, RHODE ISLAND, ON SAKONNET POINT ROAD

*Kindness of Miss   Photograph by Bachrach
Clara Endicott Sears*

KING PHILIP'S WAR CLUB, OR "BATON" OF AUTHORITY

Preserved through generations in one family since the year he was killed in the Swamp Fight in 1676. It is now in the collection at the American Indian Museum at Harvard, Massachusetts — a part of "Fruitlands and the Wayside Museums Inc."— founded by Clara Endicott Sears of Harvard and Boston.

Kindness of the late E. M. Parker

SITE OF THE MYLES GARRISON HOUSE

The inscription reads: "Near this spot stood the John Myles Garrison House the place of meeting of the troops of Massachusetts Bay and Plymouth Colonies commanded by Majors Thomas Savage and James Cudworth who marched to the relief of Swansea at the opening of King Philip's War A. D. 1675." This was the beginning of King Philip's war.

Kindness of John W. Haley

GRAVES OF BENJAMIN CHURCH, THE GREAT INDIAN COLONIAL FIGHTER, AND HIS WIFE ALICE SOUTHWORTH, AT LITTLE COMP-TON, RHODE ISLAND

After having fought warlike Indians for a large part of his life, he died from a fall from his horse while returning from a visit to his sister.

Kindness of John W. Haley

DRUM ROCK IN CITY OF WARWICK,
RHODE ISLAND

An important signal device of the Narragansett Indians. Rather difficult to locate, it is a short distance west of Route 1 from Providence to Wickford, in Cowesett, south of Apponaug.

Kindness of John W. Haley

TABLET AT SITE OF THE RICHARD SMITH BLOCKHOUSE AT WICKFORD COVE, RHODE ISLAND

Where forty unfortunate colonists, killed in the Great Swamp fight at South Kingston, or who died on the return march, were buried. The situation is a beautiful one. The place is now known as Cocumcussoc and the ancient structure there is believed to have been erected upon the original foundations of the Smith blockhouse.

Kindness of John W. Haley

REMAINS OF THE QUEEN'S FORT, OR HIDING PLACE
IN EXETER, RHODE ISLAND

Situated about one and a half miles northwest of Wickford Junction, in the northeast corner of the town of Exeter. Here Queen Quiaiapen, a female chief of the Narragansetts, known also as Matantuck or Magnus, concealed herself from attack. The lines of the fort can still be seen, and somewhere adjoining was once the Queen's bedchamber. This Indian fort is an object of much interest.

Kindness of Clarence E. Sherman,
Librarian, Providence Public Library

From a painting owned by the Ancient and
Honorable Artillery Co. by W. S. Savory

THE GREAT SWAMP FIGHT BETWEEN THE COLONISTS AND A LARGE BAND OF INDIANS, FOUGHT ON SUNDAY, DECEMBER 19, 1675, AT SOUTH KINGSTON, RHODE ISLAND

This was a very important battle of the world, as it decided who was to dominate these lands.

Kindness of John W. Haley

GREAT SWAMP FIGHT MONUMENT, SOUTH KINGSTON, RHODE ISLAND

This spot may now be reached conveniently via the new road leading from South County Trail (Route 2), not more than a mile south of the rotary traffic circle at West Kingston.

Kindness of John W. Haley

TABLET ON THE SITE OF THE GREAT SWAMP FIGHT AT SOUTH KINGSTON, RHODE ISLAND

Placed to the memory of Major Samuel Appleton of Ipswich, Massachusetts, who was greatly responsible for the victory of the colonists.

Kindness of Francis I. McCanna

INDIAN CHURCH IN THE NARRAGANSETT RESERVATION AT CHARLES-TOWN, ONCE A PART OF WESTERLY, RHODE ISLAND, ABOUT TWELVE MILES SOUTH OF NARRAGANSETT

An earlier building was erected in 1750, the present one, built by the Narragansett Indians, dating about a hundred years later. A few years ago the Indians living on the Reservation abandoned their simple dwellings and became scattered. At the present day, powwows are held on Sundays in front of the church. Behind the church is their graveyard, where the ancestors of one of our guides, F. M. Nichols, are buried, descendants of the great Narragansetts. A narrow wood road leads to this now deserted spot.

Kindness of John W. Haley

TABLET ON THE SITE OF THE GREAT SWAMP FIGHT, AT SOUTH KINGSTON, RHODE ISLAND

Where the "Narragansett Indians made their last stand in King Philip's War and were crushed by the United Forces of the Massachusetts, Connecticut and Plymouth Colonies in the Great Swamp Fight, Sunday, 19 December 1675."

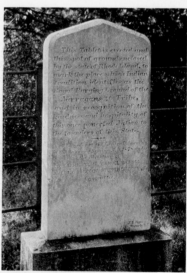

Kindness of Francis I. McCanna

TABLET IN THE ROYAL BURIAL GROUND OF THE NARRAGANSETTS AT TOWER HILL, CHARLESTOWN, RHODE ISLAND

Kindness of Francis I. McCanna

FORT NINIGRET ENCLOSING BURIAL GROUND, CHARLESTOWN,
RHODE ISLAND

Situated about twelve miles south of Narragansett, of more recent date than the Royal
Burial Ground not far away. Its location is at Fort Neck, overlooking Ninigret Pond.
Within the compound is a memorial boulder placed to the memory of the Narragansett and
Niantic Indians, "the unwavering friends and allies of our fathers."

Kindness of Francis I. McCanna

ROYAL BURIAL GROUND OF THE NARRAGANSETT TRIBE AT TOWER HILL,
CHARLESTOWN, RHODE ISLAND

Where lie the remains of the Kings, Queens, members of the Royal Family and Chieftains
of the Narragansetts. It is situated one mile north of the Post Road. This plateau is
situated in an attractive spot overlooking the ocean in the distance.

From "A Popular History of the United States," Vol. III, by William Cullen Bryant and Sydney Howard Gay

Reproduced by permission of Charles Scribner's Sons, New York

ESTHER KENYON, THE LAST OF THE ROYAL NARRAGANSETTS, AND SISTER OF "KING TOM" NINIGRET

She was the last of the tribe to be crowned here. An eye witness wrote: "When the crown was put on the soldiers fired a royal salute, and huzzaed in the Indian tongue. The ceremony was imposing."

Kindness of H. W. Dorsey

From Smithsonian Institute Bureau of American Ethnology, Washington, D.C.

PHILIP, ALIAS METACOMET, OF POKANOKET

Kindness of John W. Haley

THE PIPE OF POMHAM

Kindness of Francis I. McCanna

ROCK AND TABLET AT FORT NINIGRET, CHARLESTOWN, RHODE ISLAND

A memorial to the Narragansett and Niantic tribes.

Kindness of Francis I. McCanna

CORONATION ROCK ON THE "KING TOM" FARM AT CHARLESTOWN, RHODE ISLAND

King Tom's sister Esther was the last of the tribe to be crowned here. The ceremony was performed with the same pomp which attended the coronation of her ancestors in the years gone by.

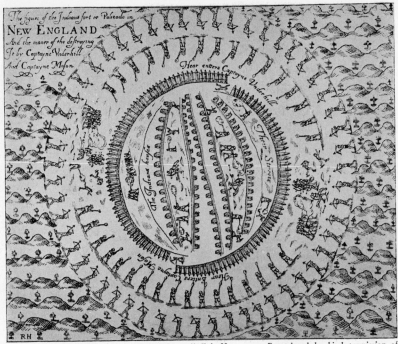

*From "A Popular History of the United States," Vol. II,
by William Cullen Bryant and Sydney Howard Gay*

*Reproduced by kind permission of
Charles Scribner's Sons, N.Y.*

ATTACK ON AND CAPTURE OF THE PEQUOT FORT AT MYSTIC, CONNECTI-
CUT, BY CAPTAINS MASON AND UNDERHILL, LEADERS OF THE COLONIAL
TROOPS IN 1637

Kindness of Ernest E. Rogers

ANCIENT HOUSE OF LUCY OCCOM
TANTAQUIDGEON, SISTER OF SAM-
SON OCCOM AND WIFE OF THE SON
OF THE FAMOUS MOHEGAN WAR-
RIOR WHO CAPTURED MIANTO-
NOMO

Several of the Indians now living nearby
are directly descended from Tantaquidgeon,
and Lucy Occom.

Kindness of Ernest E. Rogers

ORIGINAL WELL OF SAMSON OCCOM
ON THE LATE HENRY W. BAKER'S
PROPERTY IN THE MOHEGAN RES-
ERVATION

Samson Occom's house, of which a picture was reproduced in the first Indian
booklet, stood near.

From "History of the Indians of Connecticut from the Earliest Known Period to A.D. 1850," by John W. De Forest

SOUTH VIEW OF MOHEGAN CHAPEL, MONTVILLE, CONNECTICUT, ON THE RIVER THAMES BETWEEN NEW LONDON AND NORWICH

This church was remodeled and enlarged in 1831, as shown in another illustration. It is on the former Mohegan Reservation, which is now occupied by about ten families.

Kindness of Ernest E. Rogers　　　*Photographed by Mr. Bishop of the Bishop Studio of New London*

MOHEGAN CHURCH ON THE MOHEGAN RESERVATION AT MONTVILLE, CONNECTICUT — NEAR THE RIVER THAMES, BETWEEN NEW LONDON AND NORWICH

This church is the result of remodeling and enlargement in 1831 of the original building shown in the illustration above.

Kindness of Ernest E. Rogers

HOME OF THE LATE HENRY W. BAKER, A DESCEND-
ANT OF UNCAS AND LUCY OCCOM TANTAQUIDGEON
It was formerly the Mohegan schoolhouse on the east side of
the Mohegan Turnpike between New London and Norwich,
moved within a few feet of the former residence of Samson
Occom on the east side of road, and remodeled. Left to right —
the late Henry W. Baker and Ernest E. Rogers.

*Kindness of the late P. Le Roy Harwood of
New London*

CAPTAIN JOHN MASON MONUMENT
AT MYSTIC, CONNECTICUT
This statue on Pequot Hill, the site of
Pequot Fort, was unveiled on June 26,
1889, with fitting military ceremonies.
Captain Mason, a hero of the Pequot War,
died in Norwich, Connecticut, in his sev-
enty-third year.

Kindness of Ernest E. Rogers

MOHEGAN BURIAL GROUND AND FORT AT FORT SHANTOK, MONTVILLE, NOT FAR FROM THE MOHEGAN RESERVATION. IT IS SITUATED IN A FIELD OVERLOOKING THE BEAUTIFUL THAMES RIVER

Here was the Indian Trading Cove and the site of the Mohegan Village and stronghold of Uncas. The burial ground situated in the 160 acres acquired by Fort Shantok State Park is surrounded by a palisade built in Indian fashion.

Kindness of Earle W. Stamm

THE VERY IMPRESSIVE BURIAL GROUND OF THE MOHEGANS ON SACHEM STREET IN THE CENTER OF THE TOWN OF NORWICH, CONNECTICUT, CALLED THE CITY OF THE KINGS. THE TALL MONUMENT IS PLACED OVER THE GRAVE OF UNCAS, THE CELEBRATED CHIEFTAIN OF THE MOHEGANS

There is also a memorial stone to Mamohet, who died in England in 1735. The grave-stone of Samuel Uncas, a descendant, and one of the last of the Sachems, is in the Slater Memorial Building.

Kindness of Arthur L. Peale and Earle W. Stamm

MONUMENT ERECTED TO THE NAR-
RAGANSETT CHIEFTAIN MIANTO-
NOMO (1643) ON SACHEM PLAIN IN
GREENVILLE, OUTSIDE OF THE CITY
OF NORWICH, CONNECTICUT

Its approach is through the attractive
Mohegan Park.

Kindness of Ernest E. Rogers

CAIRN IN THE SHAPE OF A WIGWAM
IN THE MOHEGAN CEMETERY NEAR
THE MOHEGAN RESERVATION ON
THE RIVER THAMES

It is known as the Leffingwell Memo-
rial, and is placed at Uncas' Fort known as
Fort Shantok. On the cairn is an inscrip-
tion stating, "Here stood the fort of Uncas
Sachem of the Mohegans and friend of the
English; here in 1645 when besieged by the
Narragansetts he was relieved by the brav-
ery of Lt. T. L. Leffingwell." This ceme-
tery is now included in Fort Shantok State
Park.

*Kindness of Mrs. Ozias Dodge, Director of The
Slater Memorial Museum, Norwich, Connecticut*

SUCCOTASH BOWL OF UNCAS IN THE
MEMORIAL MUSEUM OF NORWICH,
CONNECTICUT

*From "History of Norwich, Connecticut, from its Settlement in 1660,
to January 1845," by Miss F. M. Caulkins*

"INDIAN LEAP" AT NORWICH OR YANTIC FALLS, IN
NORWICH, CONNECTICUT, WHERE THE YANTIC RIVER
JOINS THE SHETUCKET RIVER

The Mohegans in 1643 chased many of the Narragansetts
over the falls to their death.

BUFFALO BILL (COLONEL WILLIAM F. CODY) WITH CHIEFS IRON TAIL AND
ROCKY BEAR OF THE SIOUX TRIBE, AND ONE HUNDRED MOUNTED INDIAN
BRAVES, AT THE UNCAS MONUMENT, NORWICH, CONN., JULY 2, 1907, HOLD-
ING A MEMORIAL SERVICE.

Kindness of Earle W. Stamm
MONUMENT AT GREAT PLAINS IN
THE WESTERN PART OF NORWICH,
CONNECTICUT, COMMEMORATING
ONE OF THE GREATEST OF PURELY
INDIAN BATTLES FOUGHT BE-
TWEEN THE MOHEGANS, UNDER
UNCAS, AND THE NARRAGANSETTS,
COMMANDED BY MIANTONOMO
The latter was captured by Tantaquid-
geon, a Mohegan, whose descendants today
live in the former Mohegan Reservation.

the mark  of UNCAS.